Praise for

LEADERSHIP
Is a Life Skill

M000238706

"I have had numerous coaches throughout my athletic and business careers; however, very few individuals have been as clear and profound in their coaching as Mariam MacGregor. Leadership is in her DNA. You will get timely insights from her book *Leadership Is a Life Skill*. This content is essential for anyone interested in unleashing leadership potential within our children. Mariam's work has made measurable improvements in both my personal and professional lives."

—Cedric James, director of TCU IdeaFactory, K–12 student mentor, and former NFL athlete

"*Leadership Is a Life Skill* is a great resource for anyone who works with children and teens. Mariam brilliantly demonstrates the need for teaching and modeling leadership skills, and her process for performing an audit to find the missing pieces in each school or group working with adolescents is easy to do and applicable across the board. As the executive director of an organization who has benefited firsthand from Mariam's insight and coaching, her tools and guidelines are relevant in preparing students, educators, and schools for necessary skill sets personally and professionally. When students are taught that everyone has a place at the table, it shifts the dynamic to value and collaboration."

—Kristin Steadman, founder and executive director of Night Lights

"*Leadership Is a Life Skill* is a thoughtful guide for cultivating a leadership culture that will benefit students of all abilities. As a mother of a child with multiple disabilities, I am encouraged by the inclusive strategies and activities Mariam presents to support and develop confident, tolerant, and empathetic current and future leaders in our schools and communities."

—**Jocalyn Briggs,** certified teacher for students with visual impairments, inclusion specialist, and disability advocate

"If you are looking for a book to transform your school system, this is it. Practical, thoughtful, comprehensive, informative, helpful, positive, and personal, *Leadership Is a Life Skill* will help you make a difference at the ground level whether you are a student, teacher, staff, administrator, parent, or board member."

—**Barry Z. Posner, Ph.D.,** professor of leadership, Leavey School of Business, Santa Clara University, and coauthor of *The Leadership Challenge*

"*Leadership Is a Life Skill* provides the blueprint to develop leadership as a school-wide focus, which will yield ongoing benefits to individuals and to communities. Launching young people on a lifetime of effective leadership is a game changer."

—**Dr. Julia Link Roberts,** Mahurin Professor of Gifted Studies, Western Kentucky University

LEADERSHIP

Is a Life Skill

Preparing Every Student to Lead and Succeed

Mariam G. MacGregor, M.S.

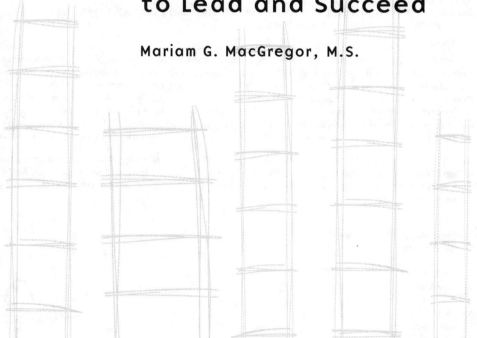

free spirit
PUBLISHING®

Copyright © 2018 by Mariam G. MacGregor, M.S.

All rights reserved under International and Pan-American Convention. Unless otherwise noted, no part of this book may be reproduced, stored in a retrieval system, or transmitted in any form or by any means, electronic, mechanical, photocopying, recording or otherwise, without express written permission of the publisher, except for brief quotations or critical reviews. For more information, go to www.freespirit.com/permissions.

Free Spirit, Free Spirit Publishing, and associated logos are trademarks and/or registered trademarks of Free Spirit Publishing Inc. A complete listing of our logos and trademarks is available at www.freespirit.com.

Library of Congress Cataloging-in-Publication Data
Names: MacGregor, Mariam G., author.
Title: Leadership is a life skill : preparing every student to lead and succeed / by Mariam G. MacGregor, M.S.
Description: Minneapolis, MN : Free Spirit Publishing Inc., 2018. | Includes bibliographical references and index.
Identifiers: LCCN 2017060941 (print) | LCCN 2018005435 (ebook) | ISBN 9781631982491 (Web PDF) | ISBN 9781631982507 (ePub) | ISBN 9781631982484 (pbk.) | ISBN 1631982486 (pbk.)
Subjects: LCSH: Leadership—Study and teaching—United States. | Life skills—Study and teaching—United States. | Leadership in children.
Classification: LCC HM1261 (ebook) | LCC HM1261 .M325 2018 (print) | DDC 303.3/4083—dc23
LC record available at https://lccn.loc.gov/2017060941

Free Spirit Publishing does not have control over or assume responsibility for author or third-party websites and their content. At the time of this book's publication, all facts and figures cited within are the most current available. All telephone numbers, addresses, and website URLs are accurate and active; all publications, organizations, websites, and other resources exist as described in this book; and all have been verified as of June 2018. If you find an error or believe that a resource listed here is not as described, please contact Free Spirit Publishing. Parents, teachers, and other adults: We strongly urge you to monitor children's use of the internet.

The digital activities "Squeeze," "Puzzle," "Campaign Teams," "What's in a Name?," "House of Cards," "Floating Pipeline," and "Zapping Maze" first appeared in *Building Everyday Leadership in All Kids* and/or *Teambuilding with Teens* by Mariam G. MacGregor, M.S. (Minneapolis: Free Spirit Publishing, 2013, 2008), and are used here with permission of the publisher.

Cover and book design by Shannon Pourciau
Edited by Eric Braun

10 9 8 7 6 5 4 3 2 1
Printed in the United States of America

Free Spirit Publishing Inc.
6325 Sandburg Road, Suite 100
Minneapolis, MN 55427-3674
(612) 338-2068
help4kids@freespirit.com
www.freespirit.com

FSC
www.fsc.org
MIX
Paper from
responsible sources
FSC® C005010

Free Spirit offers competitive pricing.
Contact edsales@freespirit.com for pricing information
on multiple quantity purchases.

Dedicated to everyday leaders who recognize their higher purpose:
"It's not about me!"
Carry on with integrity, civility, and grace to develop next-generation leaders who continue to positively change the world.

And deep appreciation to the educators and students who so generously shared their stories.

Contents

PART 1: GETTING STARTED 11

PART 2: CREATING A CULTURE OF LEADERSHIP

ADDITIONAL RESOURCES 133

LIST OF REPRODUCIBLE FORMS

See page 157 for instructions on how to download the digital forms.

Digital Content Only

Squeeze

Puzzle

Campaign Teams

What's in a Name?

House of Cards

Olympic Rings

Floating Pipeline

Zapping Maze

Candlestick Relay

INTRODUCTION
Why Leadership Matters

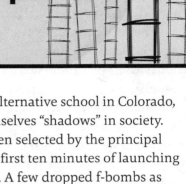

Nothing had prepared me for my first day at an alternative school in Colorado, teaching leadership to kids who considered themselves "shadows" in society. Thirty-two students sat in front of me, having been selected by the principal because of their leadership potential. Within the first ten minutes of launching the lesson, half of them stood up and walked out. A few dropped f-bombs as they exited the room, in disbelief about having to "do work" on the first day and seeing no value in the class. My heart dropped like those curse words!

What have I gotten myself into? I calmly responded to each student who left, "I appreciate the short time we spent together." From the corner of my eye, I saw smirks on the faces of a few of the students who stayed.

I quickly realized that those who left perceived "leaders" as students who ran for (and won) student council positions, led athletic teams, or were chosen to help adult leaders in the school or community: goody-goodies, sellouts, and conformers. To them, the idea that someone (and the principal of all people) considered *them* leaders—and really, the overall idea of leadership—was *not* a good thing!

These teens, who for various reasons felt disengaged from school experiences, considered peers who were athletes and joiners and popular or, rather, campus social influencers, as anti-*everything* to their own experiences. For them, being considered a leader reduced their credibility—not with adults or the popular or typical crowd—but with others who were struggling in life, the ones who partied the hardest or shared their pain and brokenness. The ones causing trouble because they thought it was cool or believed they had nothing to lose. Participating in a class to make them better leaders was a waste of time.

By the end of the hour, the sixteen students who'd stayed sat in small groups, engaged in the activity I'd created for the first day—defining *leadership*. As we closed the discussion, one of the students looked at me earnestly and said, "Those people who left—they don't know what they're missing." She went on to explain that although students like her (and them) didn't fit the stereotype they associated with being a leader, after just one hour in the class, she realized how wrong she had been. Her reaction has stayed with me all these years.

The class didn't only teach leadership content. Students were invited to serve on school committees, run "Possibilities" (a weekly all-school motivational assembly), influence school policies, and participate in unique leadership-related activities like visits with local mayors and mentoring at-risk middle schoolers. Over the next few academic quarters, each of the sixteen students who had walked out at the start of that first day returned to take what became known as the "Leadership I" class after seeing what their peers got to do. When compared to the overall student population at the school, students who enrolled in the leadership class at any time over the three years I taught it had higher GPAs, a greater likelihood of graduating on time, and an increased sense of civic duty (read about an ambitious student-led community event at this school on page 97). By the time I left that school, there were four leadership classes initiated by student demand: Leadership I, Leadership II, Community Leadership (focused on social change and civic responsibility), and Advanced Leadership (focused on community impact projects).

When that student told me that she and her peers were wrong to think they couldn't be leaders, she was barely scratching the surface of how right she was. Looking back on my time with that group of students—their desire to explore leadership despite feeling overlooked and undervalued in school and in the community—I see that it changed me too. It shaped my perspective on the importance of cultivating leadership in every student, every educator, *everyone* seeking to bring his or her best self to life.

Every Student Can Lead

I've been heavily immersed in the field of leadership development for many years now, from many different angles. I've taught leadership classes to middle and high schoolers, selected and trained youth volunteers ages 10 to 17, and coordinated annual leadership events and mentoring programs in elementary schools. I've advised college students serving as organizational leaders and college students embarking on their first internships and full-time jobs. My position in higher education includes coaching college students, staff, and faculty to maximize personal awareness, build team leadership skills, and implement organizational strategies toward a leadership-driven, engaged campus and workplace. I continue to work as a leadership consultant dedicated to helping K–12 schools, colleges, and organizations develop better leadership programs for their people.

Beyond helping organizations design better programs that reach, teach, and support more leaders, my commitment to developing lifelong leaders has resulted in the Building Everyday Leadership curriculum series (for kids and teens at every grade level) and the *Teambuilding with Teens* activities guide. I reference these resources occasionally throughout this book because they provide practical, easy-to-execute sessions for a variety of classroom and student activities sessions. *Leadership Is a Life Skill* came about because the questions administrators and classroom educators most often ask me are about how to go beyond teaching a lesson or two or five throughout the year to finding ways to address leadership development for all ages across the academic spectrum in an enduring way.

Because I have one foot in K–12 education and another in higher education and career development, I see how important it is for educators to teach for life beyond academics. I'm talking about teaching leadership skills starting with our youngest citizens. By creating settings that value and promote behaviors associated with inclusive everyday leadership, we prepare kids and young adults to be effective 21st-century leaders who get things done and engage others along the way. Treating leadership as a life skill helps young leaders learn that listening, relating, understanding, and creating personal connections with others can help them make decisions that affect the greater good of organizations, schools, businesses, communities, and countries in positive ways.

While certain students often stand out because of their natural leadership abilities, focusing leadership efforts only in their direction misses the point. Students who excel as leaders absolutely deserve access to additional opportunities inside and outside the classroom, but *all* students benefit from leadership development. School environments that "call up" every student gain long-term payoffs by nurturing the next generation of leaders in industry, education, politics, the arts, and society. And by holding grown-ups equally accountable!

While it might feel impossible, there are plenty of ways to find time and resources during school days and co-curricular activities to build everyday leaders. This book shows you how it's possible and how you can do it in your school or district.

Creating Leadership Cultures in Schools

Leadership Is a Life Skill is primarily for K–12 administrators and district leaders, but classroom teachers and instructional leaders can use it to great effect on a smaller scale. Those of you in these important groups are front-and-center influencers and role models, and you are the ones in a position to inspire leadership behavior and attitudes in students, teachers, colleagues, and parents.

It's common knowledge that 21st-century education models in the United States rely too heavily on compliance and standardized testing, both of which limit student engagement and voice. The drill-and-kill culture fails to ignite valuable critical thinking skills and squeezes out opportunities to promote strong interpersonal skills needed to equip young people as citizen leaders. Developing socially and emotionally mature leaders relies on encouraging young people to act with conviction, compassion, and resourcefulness to reach goals—on their own and with teams. These benchmarks are measured by students' abilities to color outside the bubbles, not fill them in!

Research from TalentSmart, a recognized expert on emotional intelligence (EQ), shows that 90 percent of top performers have high EQs. In other words, top performers know how to use their own emotional awareness and awareness of others to successfully manage interactions. These are the "soft skills" of leadership in action. People with high EQs make $29,000 more annually than people with low EQs, and increasing one's EQ even a little can add thousands of dollars to a person's salary.[1]

While young people might not grasp the importance of EQ for their futures, as adults we recognize that developing leadership skills can serve as the conduit for demonstrating EQ (sometimes also referred to as social intelligence), and therefore deserves the same time and attention we give to athletics, music, and any other talent area, because it pays off. And unlike athletics—where

---

1. "About Emotional Intelligence," TalentSmart (2011), www.talentsmart.com/media/uploads/pdfs/About%20Emotional%20 Intelligence.pdf.

many kids envision becoming professional athletes despite the reality that only "1 percent of 1 percent" will succeed—when it comes to leadership, there's no NFL to strive for. *Everyone* has the potential to "go pro" in this arena.

On a small scale, building leadership cultures in schools launches individuals who understand the greater good into a future of leading in their homes, careers, or communities. On a larger scale, these individuals will lead school districts, large companies, cities or states, and occasionally countries.

It may feel overwhelming to be encouraged to create leadership classrooms when standardized testing and reform so heavily drive educational accountability and short-term decisions. But a culture of leadership builds competencies that inspire students to more consistently achieve their best. This means student learning and school enjoyment improve regardless of test scores.

Good educators know that students of every age and ability thrive when their "whole person" is nurtured and engaged throughout the day. A school with a leadership culture is a school with a stimulating, whole-person environment. Students enjoy school more—and get more out of it—when characteristics of leadership cultures like the following are present:

- Students can express their voices and feel heard.
- They have choices.
- They have opportunities to learn from hands-on, brain-stimulating experiences.
- Lessons relate to real-life application.
- Time is spent pondering innovative ideas.
- Time is allocated for applying critical thinking in non-rushed ways.
- Students can engage in thoughtful problem-solving with room for mistakes.
- Students feel connected to subject matter content as well as a shared sense of community with classmates.
- They have mutually respectful relationships with peers and adults who support success.
- They are challenged to strive regardless of circumstances.
- They are encouraged to do more for others.

By working to establish a leadership culture in school, we not only prepare students for a more successful future, we also make school a more positive, fulfilling, meaningful, and pleasant place to be—for everyone.

How to Use This Book

Leadership Is a Life Skill is divided into three parts. Part 1 prepares you for the hard work of transforming your school into a place where leadership is built into the foundation. Chapter 1 defines leadership and describes how leadership skills benefit your school in the short and long term, and how they benefit students for a lifetime. Chapter 2 leads you through an inventory of everything you're already doing with leadership education at your school, from classroom academics to student government, from leadership classes to SEL instruction, from athletics to clubs, and more. With that information in hand, chapter 3 leads you through the process of deciding exactly where and how you will work to make change. Your school will certainly be doing some things well already and need work in others. The Leadership Blueprint you create will include immediate changes as well as longer-term changes that will affect students in all grades. You'll find the "Leadership Blueprint at a Glance" form on pages 52–53 that you can use to help you plan it out. I recommend you read all three chapters because you'll be guided to honestly evaluate what your school is doing well and where current efforts fall short.

Once done with defining and evaluating, part 2 provides strategies, tips, and guidance for making changes in a particular area of your school. While you may already have certain programs in place, these chapters provide guidance on how to integrate leadership more intentionally into classes and activities.

- **Chapter 4: School Climate and Environment** addresses some of the questions posed during your inventory, like preparing teachers as change agents, creating a school mission or motto, and revamping orientation.

- **Chapter 5: Subject Academics and Classroom Dynamics** covers ways to infuse leadership into existing content areas.

- **Chapter 6: Teams, Clubs, and Student-Driven Leadership** explores methods for putting leadership development at the forefront of students' outside classroom activities.

- **Chapter 7: Student Support Programs and General Social-Emotional Learning (SEL)** looks at how to strengthen SEL through leadership development and vice versa.

You can read the chapters and sections of part 2 as you need them. If proposing a comprehensive and complete transformation, you'll want to read every chapter, but you can do so in any order. For example, if through your Leadership Blueprint you identify an immediate and pressing leadership need associated with student clubs and organizations, jump to Chapter 6: Teams, Clubs, and Student-Driven Leadership first.

Part 3 is full of tips and ideas to help you be a more effective leader of students and other stakeholders. It can be helpful to read both chapters early in your process and refer to them regularly as you make your way through the stages of change at your school or schools.

- **Chapter 8: Helping Students Link Leadership to Life** helps educators help students see the connection between the leadership they learn at school and their future life choices.

- **Chapter 9: Tips to Be a Transformative Leader** also includes tips geared to helping you stay organized, sharp, focused, and open-minded during what can be a big (and sometimes resisted) change. These are my tried-and-true tips for personal success as a transformational leader.

The additional resources included at the end of the book provide an example of a parent/community member handout you might send to families explaining why your school or district is choosing to prioritize leadership education. Instructions for creating a leadership sticker chart are included to help integrate leadership behaviors and expectations in classrooms with younger students. You'll also find an outline for an annual Leadership Day and a small collection of leadership lessons aligned with different academic content areas.

In addition to weaving leadership into daily lessons, discussions, behavior standards, and decision-making, what differentiates schools where leadership shapes the day from other schools? Are different core subject areas being taught? No. Are educators allocating instructional minutes differently? Maybe. Are the culture, atmosphere, and outcomes of student engagement and self-advocacy different? Yes. Are adults working in that environment being mindful as leaders and bringing their personal best every day? Yes.

When we take on the challenges of developing leadership cultures in our schools, we embrace a long view in which everyone has leadership capabilities. Kids who learn early in life the importance of relationship-building, while also gaining skills in communication, ethical decision-making, problem-solving, creative thinking, appropriate risk-taking (and mistake-making), and resourcefulness, are well on their way to building social-emotional confidence today for college and career competence later.

I hope this book inspires you to spread the lessons of leadership and that you'll reach out to me with questions or stories you want to share. You can reach me at help4kids@freespirit.com.

Mariam G. MacGregor

ONE

PART 1
GETTING STARTED

CHAPTER 1
A Hard Look at Soft Skills

More than 55 million students are enrolled in public and private K–12 schools in the United States. That's a lot of young humans having to interact with one another every day! It's hard to get along with others daily, but learning to get along *well* is important for long-term success, whether at college or in the workplace. Getting hired, promoted, or fired often depends on what it's like to work with or be with you—on teams, during meal times, during social events, as a roommate, and more.

Imagine a teenager in her first job wanting to show initiative but lacking confidence in her ability to speak up. Imagine selecting a CEO based only on contributions to the bottom line despite that person being difficult to work with or behaving in ways that make others uncomfortable. Or putting a high school quarterback into a game when team members don't trust or respect him off the field. What's missing for each of these individuals is soft skills, which can hold back even those with the brightest gifts in other areas. In our schools, we spend many hours teaching technical and academic content, yet we spend very little time developing soft skills—the important combination of social-emotional awareness and leadership skills.

Soft skills separate a book-smart person who's uncomfortable engaging in everyday conversations from an intelligent leader who makes *others* feel like the smartest person in the room. Soft skills can open doors for young leaders, even—and sometimes *especially*—if they make mistakes along the way, because people still feel valued when they interact. Soft skills represent a combination of interpersonal skills and character traits that help people successfully navigate working with others. Sometimes these skills are obvious, like when a person is a natural group leader or a magnetic public speaker. Sometimes people demonstrate soft skills in intangible ways just by their nature—they seem at ease with themselves and interact so effortlessly with others.

To many, the phrase *soft skills* may not truly capture the importance of all the proficiencies it represents in the social-emotional arena. In fact, even executives struggle with this submissive-sounding phrase. The term *leadership* sounds beefier, more quantifiable, and more tangible. Whatever we call them, this book is about developing lifelong interpersonal skills that help prepare students to work well with others over their lifetimes. Colleges, companies, and communities are seeking students who possess these skills and who can contribute positively to teams.

When I use the term *leadership skills* in this book, I am referring to a broad range of soft skills that includes social-emotional competency and interpersonal skills with an emphasis on the ability to use those skills in any social or formal situation to bring people together, find solutions as part of a team, and succeed personally. More specifically, this book is about preparing students to feel confident using their skills to serve as leaders in the wide range of situations they'll encounter in school and life.

The Connection Between Leadership Skills and Future Success

Research supports the connection between leadership skills and success. Students who build leadership skills tend to have higher attendance rates, increased empathy, greater confidence to speak up, and increased interest in postsecondary or vocational training programs. The Collaborative for Academic, Social, and Emotional Learning (CASEL), an internationally recognized organization focused on integrating academic, social, and emotional learning in the K–12 experience, identifies five core competencies that coincide directly with characteristics of socially intelligent leaders: self-awareness, self-management, social awareness, relationship skills, and responsible decision-making. CASEL's research reinforces that skills in these areas are learnable. Therefore, creating a whole-school culture of leadership makes sense if we want to develop socially competent students.

Research done by organizational development powerhouse Deloitte Consulting indicates that adaptive leadership skills and "leadership agility" (the ability for teams to innovate at high speed) are critical skills to develop when preparing for the workforce. This research, conducted biannually and consisting of a survey of more than 10,000 business and HR leaders from 140 countries, shows that 42 percent of companies surveyed in 2017 claimed leadership development is important.[2] Millennial employees agree: A majority start work seeking mentorship and flexible, on-the-job opportunities to engage and lead teams. Knowing this, educators must commit to better preparing current students for a rapidly changing workplace.

Though the workplace surely feels far off to kids, teaching them to develop and refine their leadership skills *now* will help them be ready *later*—which will come sooner than they know it. For kids who go on to college, leadership skills will help them excel there. For some kids, high school is the last of their formal education. If we want to prepare them to compete in the workplace with college graduates, they deserve sufficient leadership development early on. My interactions with thousands of students from kindergarten through college has revealed one thing—young people who master these skills do better in college and careers than those who don't.

The *Future of Jobs* report issued by the World Economic Forum—the international expert on state-of-the-world research—pointedly shows development areas where we may be falling short in preparing kids for their future workplaces. This data comes from a survey of human resources and other "senior talent and strategy executives of leading global employers, representing more than 13 million employees across nine broad industry sectors in fifteen major developed and emerging economies and regional economic areas."[3]

---

2. "2017 Deloitte Global Human Capital Trends," Deloitte University Press (2017), www2.deloitte.com/us/en/pages/human-capital/articles/introduction-human-capital-trends.html.
3. *The Future of Jobs*, World Economic Forum (2016), www3.weforum.org/docs/WEF_Future_of_Jobs.pdf.

Top 10 Workplace Skills Needed *(ranked by most important first)*[4]	
2015	**2020**
Complex Problem-Solving	Complex Problem-Solving
Coordinating with Others	Critical Thinking
People Management	Creativity
Critical Thinking	People Management
Creativity	Coordinating with Others
Quality Control	Emotional Intelligence
Service Orientation	Judgment and Decision-Making
Judgment and Decision-Making	Service Orientation
Active Listening	Negotiation
Creativity	Cognitive Flexibility

Both columns clearly indicate the need for educators to help students develop leadership skills. For both 2015 and 2020, complex problem-solving remains at the top. (Most educators might agree, though, that our national reliance on multiple-choice, bubble-in assessments does the opposite of encouraging critical thinking.) "People management" and "coordinating with others," leadership skills associated with the ability to influence, inspire, and transform (individually and as groups) to help organizations succeed, are in the top five for both lists.

Expecting people to possess "emotional intelligence"—new to the list for 2020—suggests a need to pay more attention to social-emotional learning in general, which is echoed by the CASEL research. "Cognitive flexibility" is the ability to mentally switch tasks or think about two different ideas at the same time. Its addition to the 2020 list inspires thoughts of growth mindset—a love of learning and the belief that gaining knowledge isn't finite—as well as adaptability and agility when faced with change. Emotional intelligence and cognitive flexiblity are just two behaviors we associate with effective leaders.

---

4. *The Future of Jobs*, World Economic Forum (2016), www3.weforum.org/docs/WEF_Future_of_Jobs.pdf.

You can imagine why traits like critical thinking and creativity will be important in the future: The workplace is changing at a rapid pace. Some jobs that existed ten years ago are gone, while others yet to be imagined hover on the horizon. Expansion of the global economy and new start-ups continue to create fast-paced job opportunities for people with adaptable leadership skills as well as technical knowledge. Amplifying kids' natural empathy and comfort with connecting with others will help them emerge as trustworthy, credible, and effective leaders in a wide range of workplaces.

More Benefits of Leadership

From 1990–1998, the W.K. Kellogg Foundation funded thirty-one projects that emphasized leadership development in young adults. Several of the programs served high schoolers or younger. In 1998, the foundation published a retrospective evaluation of the projects that is still considered seminal in leadership research. The evaluation, *Leadership in the Making: Impact and Insights from Leadership Development Programs in U.S. Colleges and Universities,* affirmed these outcomes of leadership development:[5]

- increased commitment to service and volunteerism

- improved communication skills

- higher sense of personal and social responsibility

- increased sense of civic/social/political efficacy

- improved self-esteem

- improved problem-solving ability

- increased civic/social/political activity

- increased sense of being galvanized for action

- increased desire for change

- improved ability to be issue-focused

- improved conflict resolution skills

- improved likelihood of sharing power

---

5. Zimmerman-Oster, Kathleen and John C. Burkhardt, *Leadership in the Making: Impact and Insights from Leadership Development Programs in U.S. Colleges and Universities. Executive Summary,* W.K. Kellogg Foundation (2004), www.wkkf.org/resource-directory/resource/2004/01/leadership-in-the-making-impact-and-insights-from-leadership-development-programs-in-us-colleges-and.

More than twenty years later, outcomes associated with leadership education aren't too different from the Kellogg research. For many years, I've collected information from middle and high school youth leadership programs and classes that shows students engaged as resources and partners in leadership activities at school or in their communities have:

- better attendance rates

- higher achievement and graduation rates

- greater confidence in resolving conflicts without adult intervention

- increased involvement in decision-making processes

- greater understanding of diversity and social inclusiveness

- greater confidence when speaking in (as a member) and to a group

- increased interest in and follow-through for service and "giving back" to others

- strong sense of ownership for school-related projects, programs, and efforts

These outcomes will benefit students in many ways in the long term, but they also will help students perform better in the short term—and improve the climate of your school.

Skills Associated with Leadership

You can probably find a thousand definitions of leadership, but among thought leaders, authors, and researchers on the subject, there is general agreement about the skills associated with effective leaders. The list on pages 19–22 organizes some of these within seven main categories. Though many of these leadership skills read as character traits, they are all learnable as *skills*. With practice, training, and opportunities to use them, kids of all ages can learn to be more adept with these skills.

When kids learn these leadership behaviors and characteristics early in life, the benefits are long lasting. Kids help others feel valued and connected. They create relationships and meaningful connections with others. They help others feel as if someone "gets them," so others are more willing to trust and follow them.

When you prioritize lessons, activities, programming, and campus culture efforts that address these seven categories of leadership, you'll see these skills change the immediate culture of your school while influencing people long term. That's the "why" of leadership skills training. And the more situations young people are put into where they can practice empathy as leaders, the more successfully we reinforce leadership lessons throughout the K–12 experience. That's the "how."

Next Steps: Bringing Leadership Culture to Your School

Creating leadership cultures in our schools hinges on the premise that we can teach students the qualities of socially intelligent leaders just like we can teach the lessons of any academic subject. But because life's best leadership lessons come from interacting with others, we need to go beyond classrooms and lessons and integrate leadership into social interactions, co-curricular activities, and more.

Your school or district may have teachers and programs already in place that teach leadership. Becoming a "whole leadership" school or district means reimagining it as a "Leadership School" or "Leadership District," one where leadership is built into the foundation. This takes hard work and firm commitment from you and other professionals in your school or district.

Leadership programming and education can't be done in a vacuum—constructive conversation involving multiple stakeholders along the way leads to greater programmatic and decision-making success. Integrating leadership development school- and community-wide is not fix-it-quick reform; it's forward-thinking educational redesign.

LEADERSHIP SKILLS

SELF-AWARENESS

Benevolent—approaches circumstances with trust and optimism rather than suspicion and maleficence (assumes people are motivated by good rather than evil)

Coachable—accepts guidance and feedback with an open mind

Confident—possesses an internally driven sense of self-worth; able to view self independently from others; uses introspection to gain understanding of own personality, strengths, weaknesses, motivations, and role in relationships; speaks up for one's self; communicates needs and focuses on strengths

Governing—able to control behavior and emotions in age-appropriate ways

Humble—maintains perspective on one's own importance; understands that others may be wiser, more experienced, more informed, and might disagree on a subject

WORKING WITH OTHERS

Approachable—viewed by others as friendly, warm, and agreeable

Collaborative—works well and productively with others; respectfully communicates alternate views without putting personal agendas above group goals or the common good

Engaging—attracts and involves others by modeling active participation; possesses the intuitive ability to motivate and encourage others to join an effort or cause

Encouraging—finds opportunities to promote the strengths of others, leading for success and learning rather than leading through competition, judgment, or limitation

Harmonious—learns the difference between disagreement and conflict; learns to recognize conflict; interacts with others to resolve conflicts to continue to be productive by encouraging cooperation and compromise

CONTINUED»

From *Leadership Is a Life Skill* by Mariam G. MacGregor, M.S., copyright © 2018. This page may be reproduced for individual, classroom, or small group work only. For all other uses, contact Free Spirit Publishing Inc. at www.freespirit.com/permissions.

Working with Others, continued

Inclusive—considers the needs and interests of others on teams, programs, projects, and goals

Uniting—seeks ways to bring people together and takes steps to do so; connects with others to achieve positive interactions and potentially achieve a common cause; engages in actions that bring people together; acts with authentic care, conscientiousness, and empathy that draw others to him or her

QUALITIES OF LEADERSHIP

Adaptable—capable of changing direction or approach when faced with new situations, new or contradicting information, or new challenges and priorities

Discerning—applies insight and understanding to choices, opportunities, decisions, involvements, and relationships; builds or demonstrates the capacity to be definitive (capable of saying yes or no or ask for help)

Patient—takes time when handling people, priorities, and possibilities; can handle delays without becoming anxious or attempting to control or micromanage team and time

Rational—responds to situations with sensible logic and appropriate emotional affect

Resilient—experiences and learns to accept failure; learns to rebound from challenges and crises (whether a result of team or personal efforts); applies perspective and lessons to future efforts (good attempts don't always lead to good results); can manage disappointment

Respectable—acts in manner deserving of admiration and consideration from others

Respectful—treats others politely, graciously, and with consideration

Responsible—works hard to achieve goals; can be counted on by others

Trustworthy—considered by others as honest, steadfast, transparent, and reliable; someone others can count on without worrying about underlying agendas

CONTINUED»

From *Leadership Is a Life Skill* by Mariam G. MacGregor, M.S., copyright © 2018. This page may be reproduced for individual, classroom, or small group work only. For all other uses, contact Free Spirit Publishing Inc. at www.freespirit.com/permissions.

COMMUNICATING, LISTENING, AND BEING HEARD

Attentive—engages with and learns from others by listening to understand (without scripting responses)

Consultative—gives blame-free feedback (focused on behaviors, not people); seeks ways to improve together; listens openly to feedback from others to learn, understand, and change personal behaviors as needed

Diplomatic—listens openly to opposing views and seeks to identify and determine common ground or mutual understanding in order to move forward; communicates important and necessary information to others in appropriate ways

Perceptive—conveys ideas and perspectives clearly and effectively based on setting and context, method (writing, speaking, presenting), and relationship with other person or audience

DECISION-MAKING AND PROBLEM-SOLVING

Action-Oriented—takes steps to put ideas into motion; self-motivated

Adaptable—accepts uncertainty, making decisions and building skills to successfully get through it

Analytical—thinks critically; evaluates information, ideas, problems, and situations beyond superficial levels and looks beneath the surface to understand driving forces

Assertive—takes initiative; takes steps to implement new ideas, solve problems, motivate others, find solutions, and get work done without being asked by others

Hopeful—approaches situations and circumstances (even difficult ones) with a hopeful attitude and optimistic, positive outlook; inspires others to do the same; believes good things can happen

Resourceful—finds quick and clever ways to overcome obstacles and succeed in difficult situations or circumstances

CONTINUED≫

From *Leadership Is a Life Skill* by Mariam G. MacGregor, M.S., copyright © 2018. This page may be reproduced for individual, classroom, or small group work only. For all other uses, contact Free Spirit Publishing Inc. at www.freespirit.com/permissions.

SOCIAL SOLUTIONS

Empathetic—capable of putting one's self in another person's shoes with sincerity, and of using that firsthand connection to drive conversations and decisions

Globally Aware—willing and open to seeing the world through unique filters based on individual experiences

Organizationally Committed—commits to being positive organizational contributor; has an "if not me, then who" attitude; avoids making excuses when things go wrong; aligns with norms and expectations while also willing to challenge status quo when it's unproductive to organization

Organizationally Engaged—identifies with, connects to, and gets actively involved in a team, club, school, job, or other organization; strives toward personal best individually and in teams

Service Minded—unselfish; does things for others without expecting anything in return

Upstanding—confronts others who are bullying or mistreating others; challenges behaviors or traditions that undermine supportive culture of an organization or school; acts when sees a wrong

SEEKING OPPORTUNITIES

Bold—speaks up and takes steps to challenge the status quo on behalf of others as much as oneself; willing to take the path less traveled to achieve goals

Curious—inquisitive; asks questions; embraces new ways of thinking; sees opportunity and possibility in the unknown; thinks creatively and considers "what if"

Growth-Oriented—engages in learning that stretches personal knowledge and outlook regardless of earning a grade or achieving a new benchmark

Open to Change—tries new things; accepts positive change; learns how to evaluate or improve processes; when facing resistance to change, seeks to understand why

From *Leadership Is a Life Skill* by Mariam G. MacGregor, M.S., copyright © 2018. This page may be reproduced for individual, classroom, or small group work only. For all other uses, contact Free Spirit Publishing Inc. at www.freespirit.com/permissions.

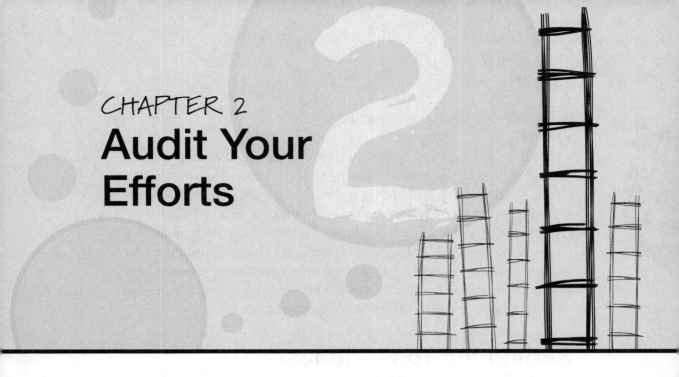

CHAPTER 2
Audit Your Efforts

Before you begin to revamp your school into one where leadership skills are valued and taught—and where leadership is inherent in the culture—it's important to get a clear idea of what you're doing already in that regard. In which areas is leadership already a strong part of the culture? In which areas could you do more?

This chapter guides you through a broad audit of how leadership is currently taught and infused in every facet of the school. Conducting the audit involves carefully and honestly evaluating existing programs, classes, co-curricular clubs, and other initiatives and elements of your school culture. This evaluation is most effective when conducted with the insights and views of multiple stakeholders, including program resources and recipients—those running programs and those who benefit.

The audit process also involves identifying in detail the actual resources involved or necessary for a program or effort to run successfully. These are the "who, what, when, where, and how" of preparing and executing leadership development—human capital, financial resources, physical and time resources, and the stamina stakeholders possess to keep a program going. To accurately evaluate each of these elements, it's valuable to select the right metrics. Because we're talking about leadership, these measurements will rely less on data points like high grades and standardized test scores and more on noticeable characteristics, attitudes, opinions, and behaviors as well as the opinions of all stakeholders.

Your finished audit will provide a focused snapshot of leadership in your school and a clearer understanding of how existing resources are being invested in developing leaders. It will also identify opportunities for program enhancements, process improvement, and innovative ways to prioritize leadership experiences for all students. Finally, it will indicate where additional resources are needed. It's easier to make decisions—big and small, short-term and long-term—when you clearly understand where current resources and programming stands. Every school is different and completing a leadership audit sets the stage to effectively work from *your* reality.

Setting the Tone: Honesty and Collaboration

Prior to initiating an audit, seek to set a tone that encourages honesty and collaboration with everyone you're engaging in this process, particularly the teachers and staff involved. While this is the natural tone in some school teams, others may have a culture of resistance, territorialism, and caution. Overcoming such an atmosphere can take time; a first step to combat apprehension or distrust is to work together beforehand with sets of stakeholders to define what leadership means in your setting.

Consider putting together a temporary committee that represents a cross section of your school—teachers, students, administrative staff, and other staff—tasked with hammering out a definition. Rather than serving as the facilitator yourself, ask the committee to identify a leader or point person to objectively manage the process. Since this committee is temporary, with one task to achieve, it's best to choose people already committed to implementing leadership in your school. Prior to reaching the final definition, you'll want to determine who has final authority to sign off on it and how to enthusiastically message the results to your school. Whatever you decide, communicate clearly and set parameters on what elements will be reflected in a "good" definition.

LEADERSHIP in ACTION

A School's Definition of Leadership

In the early 1990s, Vantage Point High School, an alternative school in Colorado, urged students and staff to formulate a definition of leadership that would promote candor and collaboration daily. When they had established their definition, they posted it generously throughout the building:

Focus on Learning, Mutual Respect, Support Each Other, Appropriately Confront

To continue to represent how students, staff, and parents work together, the staff and students regularly revisit their leadership definition and the terms agreed upon many years ago.

The thoughtfulness involved in community-developed definitions serves as a reminder for everyone to pay attention to how your school is truly building leadership skills, behaviors, and competencies across the curriculum as you implement change. It helps establish the idea that *we're all on the same team,* reducing tension along the path toward rooting your school in leadership and achieving the academic and social/emotional growth you expect at every grade level.

On page 59 in chapter 4, you'll also find a section on creating a leadership definition or school motto with your stakeholders as a way of improving school climate and environment. You may want to revisit the process at that point even if you establish a working definition prior to your audit or keep this definition if it has been communicated a lot and is popular and effective with your school population. You can always decide to revisit the definition process later, but there's no need to repeat it if you've created one that is working for your situation.

Starting the Audit: What to Look For

Relevant leadership development efforts likely already exist in your setting, so going through the audit can strengthen the groundwork to insure your efforts are intentional and inclusive for students at all levels. When formulating your audit, take a close look into each of the areas that follow and any others germane to your school, community, and diversity of stakeholders. Guidelines for framing and conducting your audit begin on page 31.

School Environment and Climate

A school's climate is established and perpetuated in many ways. It's everything tangible and intangible that influences a school's shared identity. In your audit, gather information about the following areas and any others that you find appropriate to your school's climate and environment.

School mission statement or motto. Does our school have one? If so, how was it created? What does it say about leadership? Does it encourage initiative, compassion, or courage? How is our mission or motto communicated to anyone who walks in our door?

Orientation programs for new students. Who creates and drives the orientation? What message does it send to new students? In what ways is leadership a part of orientation? What roles do students play in welcoming others to our school? Can student aides be trained to serve as ambassadors for student or adult visitors? How confident do new students feel after attending orientation about their first few weeks of school?

Behavior modeled by adults. Do kids look up to and respect staff? Why or why not? Which adults in your school do students admire most, and why? What leadership behaviors are expected from staff? How do we communicate and train everyone in these areas? What does personal leadership accountability look like for our staff?

Handling conflict and complex issues. What is our method for behavior management? Is it working? How would students and adults change it? Does everyone have a voice in the process? How are we building competency for all members of our community to productively handle conflict? How do we talk about difficult topics? How do we respond when someone feels we have failed in our handling of a challenging issue affecting our school community?

School-wide celebrations, traditions, and expressions of school spirit. What do we celebrate as a school, and why? What is missing—that is, what *should* we be celebrating? How do we celebrate our school? What else can we do? Does the community know about our accomplishments? How do we communicate accomplishments and opportunities to our internal and external stakeholders? What is our school amazing at? What traditions are important to our school community? How do people rank the importance of school spirit? How do we address traditions when they distract or negatively impact our school community? Are our traditions and school spirit inclusive of all students?

Condition and use of facilities and physical gathering spaces. Are students and adults comfortable at school? Are the facilities clean, up to date, and safe? Do we get the best use out of our facilities? What can we do better? What needs to be updated? Do students and staff have common areas to gather together and separately? Do students and staff feel pride about our facilities?

You may want to use some or all of the previous questions, and you'll no doubt want to formulate additional questions and discussions for each area that applies to your school. The goal is to create a welcoming, engaging, and encouraging atmosphere at your school for students, staff, and visitors of all kinds (from community members to opposing football teams).

Subject Academics and Classroom Dynamics

In your audit, it's not necessary to comb through every lesson plan. Instead, you might organize a select group of teachers representing a range of grades or subject areas—depending on the grades of your school—who are responsible for evaluating syllabi, units, or lesson themes to find ways to integrate leadership content. Keep in mind that leadership can be tied to classroom academics in two main ways: through the subject matter—by making connections to leadership in the content of lessons—as well as through *how* a class is taught and students are evaluated. Use the following questions as a guideline to explore how you're currently doing both.

- In what ways are students given ownership over learning?

- How can we structure assignments so that students use leadership skills? What alternate grading methods can we incorporate that recognize leadership behaviors and application?

- Where can leadership content easily be integrated (in certain lessons, subjects, or classes such as advisory)?

- When current events that illustrate leadership occur in the real world, are teachers given the latitude to include timely discussions of or new content related to that leadership moment? Which teachers do this well and how can their ideas be applied to other classes?

Teams, Clubs, and Student-Driven Leadership

The link between student success and involvement in activities is well researched and supported. Every athletic team and extracurricular club has its own culture and thus its own opportunity for positive leadership opportunities. This part of your audit includes:

- athletic teams (sports with tryouts and season selections such as cross-country, football, soccer, volleyball, basketball, tennis, golf, swimming and diving)

- other (nonathletic) competitive, limited-selection activities such as theater

- intramurals (ultimate Frisbee, flag football, team sports for fun)

- academic teams (math team, debate team)

- academic clubs (Spanish club, history club, art club)

- student government

- special interest and social clubs (yoga club, Lego club, coding club)

- service learning and volunteerism (Kids Care Club, Key Club)

- school services (newspaper, yearbook, literary magazine)

For each of these, evaluate how student leaders are chosen and what leadership opportunities they are given. How are students developing skills on the list of leadership skills (pages 19–22)? What are some ways these skills could be better incorporated? How are students making meaningful decisions that affect the organization?

Ask focused questions about the leadership climate of these clubs and teams. This includes looking at the selection process for participants, the leadership training provided for student leaders as well as group members, the expectations of advisors, and the standards of behavior and accountability for student leaders and participants—on campus, in the community, and when visiting other schools. Some clubs or athletics are the centerpiece of their community, so it's important to honestly discuss the role of those organizations in the school and broader community.

Student government. It's also important to audit your student government and any other recognized, positional leadership roles students may have in school. I recommend examining the organization and experience every year with the outgoing *and* incoming officers. This way, students are actively involved in recalibrating the organization to positively reflect the leadership dynamics of your school. Guide them to evaluate:

- Who do we attract to student government?

- Who typically runs for each position, and is this an accurate representation of our student body? If not, what can we do differently to attract peer influencers?

- How can we increase membership, participation, and connection to all groups in our school? (Identify which groups are least engaged with the organization: boys, girls, students of color, student athletes, students in band, students active in fine arts, nonjoiners, and so on.)

If your school does not have a student government, council, or advisory organization, determine ways to implement such a program. You can organize student government starting in third or fourth grade. For example, some schools create "Care Clubs" that bring together kids to participate in service projects and that have a structured leadership team that collects ideas, narrows locations (including serving at their own school), and makes decisions with teachers helping on scope and logistics. Some service groups, like Care Clubs, function like a modified Big Brothers/Big Sisters program (www.bbbs.org) and have high school students mentoring and serving side-by-side with younger students.

Other student-driven leadership. A great way to build leadership qualities in students is to put them in positions to work with peers and younger students in a meaningful way. Student-driven leadership frequently includes mentorship programs, buddy programs, tutoring, and other opportunities for students to be leaders with other students. Ask:

- How are students encouraged to serve others?
- What student-driven leadership opportunities would people be interested in adding? How does our school encourage and support students or student groups who initiate these new programs?
- How and when is training conducted for student leaders, and who is involved in preparing and coaching the students?

Student Support Programs and General Social-Emotional Learning

Many schools offer leadership-specific classes as well as character education, social-emotional learning (SEL), and/or anti-bullying programs. If your school offers elective classes or groups like these, you'll want to evaluate what is taught and how students put what they learn into action. If you don't offer any of these programs, use the audit to determine what type of program you should begin based on the needs and interests of stakeholders. Each of these programs represents an opportunity to introduce or increase valuable social-emotional education into the school.

Achieving a leadership culture is tied to SEL. Make it a goal that your SEL and other student-support programs are working in smooth concert with your leadership efforts. All classes or training in one area should echo and reinforce what's learned in the other. To evaluate how well you're doing this, ask questions such as the following.

- How do the classes or programs offered address the unique developmental areas for each grade or age?
- How are our programs meeting the needs of students focused on Maslow's lower levels as well as of kids striving for higher needs?
- How are support programs addressing leadership? How are leadership lessons addressing SEL?
- How are students using what they learn in these programs?

If you have a dedicated leadership class (or classes), evaluate its effectiveness too. Survey students (both those who have and who have not taken it) to understand how the class is perceived. Are students finding ways to use what they learn in class out in the "real world"? Look at the curriculum—could it use an update?

Structuring Your Audit

How you collect information about the status of each area will vary. For example, you may independently be able to answer questions in certain categories based on your knowledge of the school. But you'll probably want to engage stakeholders like teachers, staff, students, families, administrators, community members, and alumni.

Audit is the term I'm using to describe ways to collect insight. The audit will likely include surveys (on paper or using a digital survey platform like Survey Monkey or Qualtrics), a series of intentional dialogues, or the establishment of committees comprised of administrators, teachers, parents, students, and community members to investigate each category. When guiding focus groups or formulating your audit, ask people to explicitly evaluate the attributes and qualities of leadership each program, class, or initiative develops. Use the questions and guidelines on pages 26–31 as a starting point and refer to the list of seven categories of leadership competencies from chapter 1 (pages 19–22) to help keep your questions and discussions focused on specific leadership traits.

If your school currently has few leadership offerings, asking too many specific questions may feel too detailed. Instead, start with an eagle-eye view. How do your programs or classes inspire thinking about:

- vision (motivating others to a common goal)
- goal setting (personal and community)
- motivation (self and others)
- teambuilding (working with others, encouraging teamwork)
- taking action (achieving goals, making things happen, follow-through)
- developing character (responsible behavior, honesty, integrity, trustworthiness)
- communication
- conflict resolution/problem-solving

- values (personal and community)
- ethics
- appreciating differences and tolerance
- appropriate risk-taking as a leader
- public speaking (being prepared, having one's voice heard)
- civic/community awareness (being part of something larger than selves)
- finding and becoming mentors (providing mentors and/or offering opportunities for teens to serve as mentors)
- positive participation in community (service, volunteerism, meaningful positional opportunities)
- respect (personal and community)
- leadership competence (willing to take everyday leadership roles, large or small)
- understanding balanced lifestyles (health and wellness, stress and time management)

Basic Survey

The baseline set of questions at the end of this chapter (pages 34–37) can be used as is, as a general survey about your school, modified for the unique needs of your school, or modified further to address different settings such as classrooms, teams, clubs, and other groups. (See page 157 for how to download customizable versions.) Four versions of the survey are available: for lower elementary students, for upper elementary and middle school, for high school students, and for adults (including administrators, teachers, staff, parents, and members of the larger community). I recommend that you survey each group of stakeholders in the school or district you're working to change.

Your audit is complete when you feel like you have enough information to make informed decisions about where to prioritize your efforts to make changes. But you're best served if you have feedback from stakeholders about the general state of your school (perhaps using the surveys provided) and specific feedback from stakeholders involved in each of the areas laid out on pages 25–31 (and covered in detail in part 2 of this book). As discussed earlier, information for these specific areas should come from various sources, including surveys, focus groups, committees doing research, and your own observations.

Once the audit is complete, you'll have a lot of information. Then it's time to examine that information and make a blueprint for going forward—one tailored to *your* setting and *your* stakeholders.

LEADERSHIP SURVEY

EARLY ELEMENTARY

_____(name of school) will be making some changes. We want to know what you think about how kids learn about leadership. Answer each question the best you can.

1. Do you learn about leadership at school? If so, when?

2. What does leadership mean to you?

3. Do you learn about communication skills at school (such as active listening, clear writing, and public speaking)? If so, when?

4. When have you practiced teamwork?

5. What words describe you as a leader?

From *Leadership Is a Life Skill* by Mariam G. MacGregor, M.S., copyright © 2018. This page may be reproduced for individual, classroom, or small group work only. For all other uses, contact Free Spirit Publishing Inc. at www.freespirit.com/permissions.

LEADERSHIP SURVEY

UPPER ELEMENTARY/MIDDLE SCHOOL

At_____(name of school), we are working to become a school where leadership is a focus of our culture. Developing leadership skills—such as initiative, problem-solving, teamwork, and communication—helps students succeed in the future at school and at work. We believe every student can be a leader. We want to know what you think about the leadership culture at_____(name of school or specific program). Please answer each question the best you can.

1. When do you learn about leadership at school?

2. Do you think leadership is considered important here?

3. What does leadership mean to you?

4. Do you learn about communication skills such as active listening, clear writing, and public speaking at school? If so, when?

5. When and how do you get to practice being part of a team? What have you learned about teamwork?

6. In what ways can someone be a leader?

7. In what ways do you think of yourself as a leader? In what ways do others think of you as a leader?

8. What would you like to learn about leadership?

From *Leadership Is a Life Skill* by Mariam G. MacGregor, M.S., copyright © 2018. This page may be reproduced for individual, classroom, or small group work only. For all other uses, contact Free Spirit Publishing Inc. at www.freespirit.com/permissions.

LEADERSHIP SURVEY

HIGH SCHOOL

At_____(name of school), we are working to become a school where leadership is a focus of our culture. Developing leadership skills—such as initiative, problem-solving, teamwork, and communication—helps students succeed in the future at school and at work. We believe every student can be a leader. We want to know what you think about the leadership culture at_____(name of school or specific program). Please answer each question the best you can.

1. When do you learn about leadership at school?

2. Do you think leadership is considered important here?

3. How are leaders chosen? Are all kids given a chance to lead at school?

4. Do you learn about communication skills such as active listening, clear writing, and public speaking at school? If so, when?

5. Do you learn about soft skills such as social-emotional learning (SEL), character, and social skills? When?

6. When and how do you get to practice being part of a team? What have you learned about teamwork?

7. If you have learned leadership skills at school, how have you applied them outside of school?

8. What does leadership mean to you?

9. In what ways can someone be a leader?

10. In what ways do you think of yourself as a leader? In what ways do others think of you as a leader?

11. What would you like to learn about leadership?

From *Leadership Is a Life Skill* by Mariam G. MacGregor, M.S., copyright © 2018. This page may be reproduced for individual, classroom, or small group work only. For all other uses, contact Free Spirit Publishing Inc. at www.freespirit.com/permissions.

LEADERSHIP SURVEY

FOR TEACHERS, STAFF, PARENTS, AND OTHER ADULTS

_____ (name of school or program) will be undertaking changes to develop a culture of leadership. This culture will help students develop leadership skills such as initiative, problem-solving, teamwork, and communication that will create a more positive climate at school and help our students succeed in the future at school and at work. We believe every student can be a leader. We want to know what you think about the current leadership culture at_____(name of school or specific program). Please answer each question the best you can.

1. How does_____ (name of school or program) cultivate leadership skills and behaviors?

2. How does_____ (name of school or program) create opportunities for students to practice the leadership skills and behaviors they learn there?

3. How are student leaders chosen in_____(this class, team, or program)? Does this method allow for—and encourage—*all* students to lead?

4. Are student leaders given opportunities to make meaningful decisions about what happens in_____(the class, team, or program)? What are some areas where students could be given more meaningful control?

5. What message do you think students receive about leadership?

6. What message about leadership would you like students to receive?

7. When students participate in_____ (program, club, team, class), how do we help them understand and speak about leadership skills, behaviors, and expectations? How can we improve in this area?

8. Do we send the message that every student can be a leader? If not, how can we do this better?

9. What resources, support, and meaningful opportunities are students given to practice or continue learning about leadership and their roles as leaders outside_____(our program)?

From *Leadership Is a Life Skill* by Mariam G. MacGregor, M.S., copyright © 2018. This page may be reproduced for individual, classroom, or small group work only. For all other uses, contact Free Spirit Publishing Inc. at www.freespirit.com/permissions.

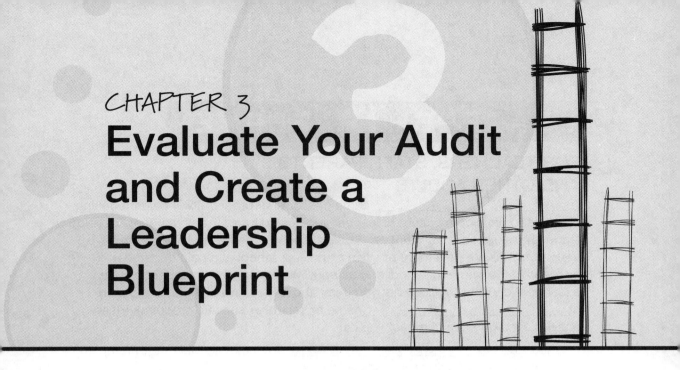

CHAPTER 3
Evaluate Your Audit and Create a Leadership Blueprint

The results from your audit set the stage for creating a leadership blueprint, the foundation of your school-wide leadership culture. Whether your audit reveals a school with a lot of leadership education or one that has a long way to go, intentionally instilling more or new leadership efforts will transform your school's culture. Most likely, you'll be asking all stakeholders to reimagine their roles. When making big changes like this, a change-management plan helps maximize visionary success.

Recruit Some Help

To implement change, establish a diverse leadership advisory team (LAT) to evaluate the audit with fresh eyes and take stock of leadership efforts, identify areas where resources and recipients overlap, and troubleshoot possible gaps. This may involve many (or all) of the same people you engaged when conducting the leadership audit. Your LAT should serve as change champions as you work together to determine how leadership efforts can take place and help you implement them. This group will be instrumental in helping you define and stick to goals, prepare for resistance, and chart your best course of action.

When determining who to recruit, be mindful that people typically fall into one of three categories when you say the word *change*. You'll want to include and give voice to people in each category:

- **Change champions** are people who move programs and changes forward. They are often the informal leaders of teachers or others on your staff. You might assume they are onboard from day one, but that's not always true—they can turn things bad quickly if they disagree with your ideas or feel like you're not listening.

- **Change resistors** are naysayers on your team, people who actively oppose forward-focused changes, dig in their heels, find comfort in the status quo, or emphasize only what could go wrong. Including change resistors helps you identify where you might face opposition or trouble spots within new programs. Resistors' hesitancy often challenges LATs to carefully examine decisions to make the smartest, most effective ones—and not just make change for change's sake. Of course, when resistors intentionally refuse to budge despite thorough analysis and overwhelming agreement, it's important not to get paralyzed by one person's extreme caution. Sometimes what's at play is irrational stubbornness or, possibly, high anxiety, not well-grounded concerns about change.

- **Change agents** are *most* people on teams. They accept change with the help of you and your change champions as you enthusiastically explain how things will be better because of the new programs, training, or activities. Change agents are successful when they deeply understand their role and have the authority to make small, meaningful impacts on their sphere of influence.

Honest communication is key to keeping people informed and excited. In my experience, the administrators most successful at creating leadership cultures communicate just as openly and candidly when things don't go as expected as when they do. If any team members are so resistant that you fear they could sabotage everyone else's success, it's imperative to coach them into *why* the change is desirable and inevitable, or to coach them *out* of your team—and into another role (at your school or elsewhere) that better fits their skillset. Chapter 4 explores some best practices in communicating your school's shift to integrating leadership as a fundamental driving force.

When making big changes, include representatives from all stakeholder groups. In general, you want a team of eight to twelve people for a single-site advisory team and twenty to thirty people for a district-wide advisory team (more if your district is extremely large; you can always divide the team into smaller, focused committees). Be certain to include voices from the following important groups of stakeholders.

Teachers

Teachers who value tangible, positive outcomes for students and colleagues are often eager to join the leadership advisory team. Ask for volunteers from your teaching staff or choose them based on who is perceived to be a leader among the teaching staff and who you believe will be enthusiastic about the changes you're making. Depending on the size of your district, select three to four teachers from each school level (elementary, middle, and high school). For a single site, select two to three teachers representing different grades.

Students

If you design an advisory team with the promise that students will get equal voice and influence as adults, it's generally easy to recruit volunteers. One way to achieve equal voice and influence is for students and adults to attend the same advisory board meetings, not create a parallel process for students.

Knowing students may be eager to join, consider implementing an application and selection process to get the most effective and diverse team members from the student population. As with teachers, seek to select student representatives from multiple grades or, in the case of a district-wide team, students from each school level with diverse experiences and perspectives that represent various concerns of unique schools. Depending on the total size of your advisory board, you will want to include two to four students. If the board represents an entire district, it's not unreasonable to include five to eight students.

Staff

Staff is a far-reaching classification. Select individuals from facility staff, school resource officers, coaches, and professional specialists such as counselors or AVID advisors (if these are separate from teachers). Many staff have dual roles, especially in smaller districts or rural schools. It's wise to choose people whose influence extends across multiple student and adult groups including frontline staff (clerical and service, custodians, bus drivers, food service), coaches, and professional staff. While frontline staff may not specifically teach leadership lessons (or teach at all), they play an important role in the culture of your school by modeling leadership, a service attitude, and relationship-building skills for students. You will want to include two to three staff members for a single site, double or triple that for a district.

Parents and Community Members

Parents and community members beyond your school board play an essential role on your LAT. They can communicate with others, promote changes taking place at your school, and serve as vocal advocates. Including community members builds a true partnership between the school and community, prevents vocal critics from functioning in a vacuum, and spreads the good news about the changes you're making. I have encountered PTA organizations that allocate a formal position as the LAT representative. This can be appealing to a parent who is motivated to positively influence the student experience beyond traditional activities associated with PTA. But enlist parents for your team beyond the PTA. Seek parents and community members who represent diverse backgrounds and school experiences, not just high achievers and natural leaders. Include three to six or more parents and community members, depending on the size of your school or district.

Administration

If you're a superintendent, then you know making change alone is impossible. If you're a principal, you may be thinking, "I don't want to make change alone!" To maintain balance and open-mindedness, look for at least two administrative representatives who have productive—and possibly unique, due to their roles or personalities—relationships with every stakeholder group represented.

It's important as the decision-making administrator that you listen to recommendations made by your LAT. Build trust with your advisory team and stay true to making leadership a school-wide priority. Don't simply put lip-service to the ideas they bring forth. If your LAT begins to feel like you're not listening or like the change they recommend won't happen, then your credibility as a leadership culture changer will be on the line.

Communicate to your LAT that you are asking them to help you do the following:

1. Review your audit to identify focus areas and create a working blueprint for transforming to a leadership culture.

2. Establish immediate changes and short- and long-term goals.

3. Get stakeholders onboard by identifying and addressing the concerns of change champions, change agents, and change resistors.

4. Collaborate on a vision for the future—the programs, classes, or other efforts you want to put into place—to build leadership for all students throughout their K–12 experience in your school or district.

5. Identify necessary training for adult and student facilitators.

6. Secure additional (or reallocate existing) resources if needed (financial, structural, human).

7. Implement the strategies identified.

Review Audit Results and Simplify Focus Areas

With your LAT, review the audit results. The results may be a mass of unorganized information, so it might help to divide it up: You could create four groups and assign each group one of the key audit areas, asking them to report to the larger group with stats and conclusions. Or you could have one group organize, summarize, and report on all parent responses, another group report on student input, and a third group report on teacher and staff input. However you break up the work, in the end, everyone on the LAT needs to have all the information at their disposal. Consider using Google Docs or another document sharing platform for raw data and for the summaries from each committee.

As you look through the feedback and information you have, remember that human nature often causes us to look at what's not happening (what we do poorly) and to ignore what's going well. Change management also prompts us to look even more critically at our gaps and misses. Knowing this, when you and your LAT review audit results early in the process, make a point of highlighting strengths and bright spots. You don't want to ignore problems, but it helps to stay positive when faced with an overwhelming amount of information, especially if much of it is negative.

One way to sort your accumulated data to hash out a direction for your efforts is to divide ideas and existing elements into *want, don't want, have,* and *don't have* categories. An easy way to do this is by drawing a diagram (see page 44) on a dry-erase board or whiteboard. The items that fall into the *Want/Don't Have* quadrant are things you may want to pursue—goals or tasks that you'll work on. Items that fall into *Want/Have* are strengths, and you'll want to keep them—though they may require improvements or changes, so they can't be totally ignored. Items that fall into *Don't Want/Have* are things you'll want to get rid of. (A typical answer here might be "students who aren't involved" or "students who feel devalued.") Like your *Want/Don't Have* items, these are action items. Finally, you may end up with some items in the *Don't Want/Don't Have* quadrant. These can be ignored.

I like to post the quadrant, pass out sticky pads, and ask everyone to write down what they believe exists in each quadrant. LAT members can place items at different points on the axes to indicate how strongly they believe the school wants or doesn't want and has or doesn't have. This can make it easier to figure out your priorities. For example, if someone puts "Reading buddies program" very high on the *Want* continuum, that means they think it is a high priority. Perhaps they also put "More parent involvement" on the *Want* continuum, but it's closer to the center of the diagram. They don't feel parent involvement is as much of a priority as a reading buddies program. Of course, multiple team members may place the same item at different points on the diagram, and all of this requires discussions.

PART I

Have/Want Diagram

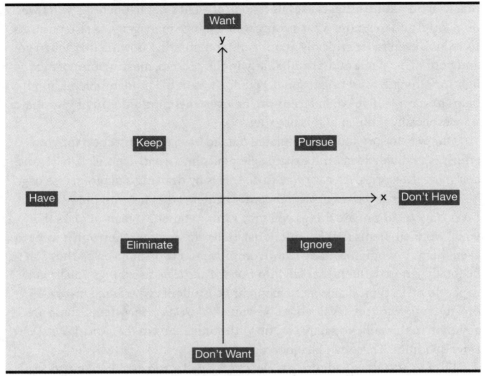

For example, imagine you're discussing your school's orientation program for kids transitioning from elementary school to middle school. The program is a hit with parents but increasingly falls flat with students, so you might put this element in the *Have/Want* quadrant. But since it needs improvement for students, you would rank it close to the center of the *Have/Don't Have* axis, indicating that it is a "Keep," but that it needs work. It is an important part of your school culture, and you are doing at least something right since the parents like it. But you want it to be a program in which new students feel engaged and get a sense that your school is a place where leadership is valued. In this case, improving the orientation program (and infusing leadership lessons and messages into it) may become a priority for you, and you can find ways to do this in Chapter 4: School Climate and Environment. Your team might suggest ideas like designing and facilitating student sessions by older students who can then serve as mentors for these same younger students during the school year. Perhaps important content can be delivered in fresh ways for today's more active and visual audiences. Or maybe the redesign of orientation results in each rising class working together to establish a leadership theme and shared values for the school year before sharing those values with the new class.

> If the Have/Want diagram doesn't seem to work for you, you can try to use a traditional SWOT analysis of your data: strengths, weaknesses, opportunities, threats. If you're unfamiliar with this method, an internet search for "SWOT" will provide plenty of guidance. However you go about the process, make it your own so it works best for you and your school or district.

In your early meetings, you will identify areas to focus on from the "Keep," "Pursue," and "Eliminate" sections of your graph. You can determine which areas to address first. Part of the equation involves considering how much work is needed to make things better, and what kind of resources are required. All these decisions are made through discussion with your LAT and will help prevent feelings of powerlessness or failure or feeling that this will never work.

Establish Short-Term and Long-Term Goals

Once your LAT has identified focus areas, consider dividing the team into smaller committees that can focus on identifying and planning for specific short- and long-term goals. The most successful goals will be tangible, actionable, quantifiable, and manageable, with action steps mapping out how to get you there. For example, if you already have a strong leadership class available as an elective, the team might set a long-term goal of having 75 percent or 100 percent of all students take the class before graduation. An action item to achieve this goal would be that the class selection system (counselors *and* your software platform) has to be able to fit all students into the class by the time they graduate.

Short-term and long-term goals can be independent of one another, or you might establish short-term goals that serve as building blocks toward achieving long-term results. Short-term goals often lead to quick wins and, therefore, nearly immediate ownership and buy-in by stakeholders. These quick wins can serve to excite your LAT because public feedback will be positive. Therefore, direct your LAT to identify at least five short-term goals that can be implemented within the school year, which is the average amount of time it takes for students to view positive experiences as tradition! For example, a short-term goal may be to host a school-sponsored Leadership Day in the spring (see page 136 for an example). Students who experience a memorable event once in their school year are more apt to say, "We do this cool event every year," even if you've conducted it only once.

As you establish your short-term and long-term goals, be sure to look at all four major areas discussed on pages 25–31: school environment and climate; subject academics and classroom dynamics; teams, clubs, and student-driven leadership (including student government); and student support programs and general SEL. You don't have to make changes in all four areas—every school or district has its own priorities and needs—but it's a good idea to examine each area to make sure you are not missing important changes that should be made.

You will also want to look at all the grades and ages of students in your school to understand how leadership is taught and infused into the culture every step of the way. Ideally, students in every grade will experience leadership lessons, training, or opportunities. Filling out the "Leadership Blueprint at a Glance" table on pages 52–53 will help you see where you may need to add services.

Create a Leadership Blueprint

To keep your LAT (and eventually your entire school community) focused on the positive changes you're implementing, create a Leadership Blueprint to show your vision for the future. The blueprint contains all the short- and long-term goals and action steps you establish. You might also list priority leadership characteristics that you want to focus on at your school (taken from the "Leadership Skills" list on pages 19–22) and, whenever you have it ready, your school's leadership definition or motto.

The Leadership Blueprint is a snapshot of what your school can be, so start with the end in mind—leadership as a life skill. The overarching goal of leadership cultures is to build long-lasting leadership attitudes in every student *now* and in preparation for the *future*. While everyone has the capacity to develop leadership skills, it may take time to get everyone interested in making leadership a priority. This is why your LAT is so instrumental in the process. They can help communicate your vision to others (teachers, parents, students, administrators) and inspire everyone to pitch in for the heavy lifting required for changes.

The blueprint helps organize your school's leadership programs, classes, clubs, trainings, and so on in a sequential, progressive, or overlapping manner based on age, grade, needs, and resources. It may help to use the "Leadership Blueprint at a Glance" form on pages 52–53 to create a handy visual reference of your desired whole-school leadership culture. The blueprint is meant to be a flexible tool that you can use in a variety of ways; fill it in with the information and details that will help you the most. Add questions you need to answer, new ideas, soft deadlines as well as hard ones, and anything else that helps you keep the big picture in focus. A sample of how to use this form is on pages 48–49.

Implementing whole-school leadership is analogous to the process many of us have experienced when implementing new educational technology platforms (for example, district-wide tablet deployment or online learning management systems). When implementing new technology, the product company will advise doing it in one of three ways: (1) piloting with a few schools or departments before implementing district-wide; (2) using a phased rollout, which allows you to activate some portions of the software and test for bugs before activating everything; or (3) "big bang"—going all in with everyone onboard from the beginning. Each of these approaches is situation-specific. Because you know your setting and your stakeholders' tolerance for change, you'll want to determine which approach is best for the level of leadership culture transformation you're inspiring.

If you're transforming a district, a pilot program might be the best way to go. You could have each of your elementary schools develop a leadership theme during the first semester to use for the year and add activities and programs to engage the students. If this program is successful, you can add the middle schools or high schools during the second semester or following

PART I

Leadership Blueprint at a Glance Sample

Name of Community/School: _____

Use this form to plan your leadership approach. You may fill in the names of existing programs (areas examined in your audit) under the grade levels they affect and add brief notes about planned changes. Include the names of programs you want to add, along with target dates for implementation. Use the "Notes" section at the bottom to list priority leadership characteristics, record your school leadership motto or definition, and any other general notes.

K	1	2	3	4	5	6
Add buddy bench by end of winter break	Add buddy bench	Add buddy bench	Add buddy bench	Add buddy bench	Add buddy bench	Middle school orientation—increase older student participation
Social skills group with 2nd/3rd-grade role model helpers	Mentored by 5th graders—start in October	Select role model helpers for K/1 social skills group	Update character ed. curriculum, more robust	Required service project—social studies, part of end-of-year assessment	Mentor 3rd graders; recruit and train early fall, start mentoring October	*How do we select older mentors? How can students help us design the session?*
	Social skills group with 2nd/3rd-grade role model helpers	*We need to develop clearer expectations and training for role models. What are our leadership competencies for students in these roles?*	Select role model helpers for K/1 social skills group	Add principal's council; recruit in November	Add principal's council	
	How do we choose who to "graduate" from this group into role models next year? What are our leadership expectations?		*We need to develop clearer expectations and training than we've had.*	Library Aides for reading skills and interactive literacy activities; discuss w/Mr. F., start week 1	Organize peer-tutoring program—work with teachers to have tutors "push-in" to classes	Add principal's council and train 6th graders for leadership roles

NOTES

Priority leadership characteristics for this year: "Working with Others" traits, especially collaborative, encouraging, inclusive, uniting.
Maybe elementary kids invite middle & high schoolers to Buddy Bench "unveiling"?

7	8	9	10	11	12
Consider adding once-a-year "navigating middle school" assembly?	Select Middle School Orientation team	Establish school motto and revise every fall	Establish school motto and revise every fall	Establish school motto and revise every fall	Establish school motto and revise every fall
Include older students on how to get involved and making good choices	Conduct training for Middle School Mentors working with 6th graders	At least 10 students involved in orientation for 8th graders coming in next year; recruit and train in April/May	Add new leadership class (required for all students for graduation), Ms. Amenope to head up	Annual workshop for coaches with Positive Coaching Alliance: August 27	Annual workshop for coaches with Positive Coaching Alliance: August 27
Add leadership class to elective choices (spring semester?)	Partner rising 9th graders with High School Ambassadors—increase meetings from 1x semester to 2x and one summer activity together by August 10	Annual workshop for coaches with Positive Coaching Alliance: August 27	Annual workshop for coaches with Positive Coaching Alliance: August 27	Select and train Playground Partners for Reynolds Elementary School	Select and train Playground Partners for Reynolds Elementary School
Create safety net for students struggling with transition to middle school (similar to younger grades social skills/leadership group)	Encourage more enrollment in leadership class—expand to 7th graders	Key Club Community Service Day (keep doing)	Key Club Community Service Day in May (keep doing)	Key Club Community Service Day in May (keep doing)	Key Club Community Service Day in May (keep doing)
How do we reach the right kids without drawing negative attention?			Select Ambassadors— have them design sessions for current 8th graders	Select Ambassadors— have them design sessions for current 8th graders	Select Ambassadors— have them design sessions for current 8th graders

NOTES

Priority leadership characteristics for this year: "Working with Others" traits, especially collaborative, encouraging, inclusive, uniting.

Re: community service day—expand list of recipient orgs to reach immigrant groups (was missing last year!)

Add academic and club accomplishments to those recognized at school assemblies year. A phased rollout might involve launching one or two elements—such as a mentor or tutoring program or an elective leadership class—district-wide, then gauging reaction and making adjustments as you add more elements in the future. Or if there is a leadership initiative you want all your high schools to implement at the same time, such as adding a leadership class to the schedule for every sophomore, you would allocate time upfront—a summer, a semester, or whatever length of time it takes to get a new course approved in your curriculum—for the designated teachers to design the leadership class. When that is complete, you'd launch the class at the start of a school year.

A big-bang approach would be much more robust. It involves making multiple changes and additions to affect multiple grades all at once. This doesn't mean you have to make every change in one year—you can, and probably will have to, implement your Leadership Blueprint over several years, increasing in reach as you go. Remember, each approach has value for the right circumstances, and the changes you're making can't (nor do they need to) happen all within a semester or a year!

Communicating for Change

For your leadership culture shift to be positively implemented, create a comprehensive communication plan both within and outside your advisory team. This means providing visible and vocal personal support in public *and* in private. For example, you can include leadership information in weekly email blasts, allocate time during staff meetings to discuss leadership topics, and create a specific logo or design for any leadership-related messaging that goes in print, on a website landing page, in email, and on any leadership "swag" (pins, pens, and bags) that you have made. This will be a visual reminder to teachers, students, and community members of your leadership goals.

When serving as a spokesperson, highlight your school's leadership theme or motto, and, as the primary representative of your school, demonstrate reliable, professional leadership. When people challenge you, be patient in trying to understand their resistance or concerns and encourage your LAT members to do the same. You all must interact with reliable, professional leadership with as many stakeholders as possible to model transparency and enthusiasm for the changes, especially with potential detractors.

It's also important that *every* stakeholder receives the same message about what is happening and why. If you're the primary influencer, work closely with your LAT to conduct town halls and open houses for different audiences. If you're working with high school students, create learning lab opportunities for students and teachers to contribute to the marketing and communication efforts—for example, graphic design classes can create the logo and associated branding, journalism or "new media" classes can put together blogs and articles, debate classes can pull together talking points and research about leadership education and soft-skills competence in the future workplace.

Similar to new product launches at major companies, you can plan TED talk–style mini-lessons, kickoff assemblies, and multi-platform social media campaigns (again, a learning lab opportunity for students on your LAT; or recruit students from the student body to put together their own committee responsible for this element).

Change doesn't happen overnight. As you take steps to shift the culture at your school, communicate clearly and often, and provide ample time and training for teachers, staff, students, and other stakeholders to gain confidence with the changes. Your LAT will thrive if you demonstrate trust by giving them the authority and influence to recommend changes and put the wheels in motion to achieve them.

Finally, remember that your Leadership Blueprint is a living document—not a static one. With time, you may find that some of your goals are no longer feasible or desirable; have the vision and flexibility to cut them. You may learn about possibilities or passions that you didn't know about before or didn't believe were important; be open-minded to adding them. Be clear in your communications about these changes, and stakeholders are likely to be onboard with them.

Part 2 of this book highlights practical strategies, tips, and ideas for achieving the goals set forth in your Leadership Blueprint.

LEADERSHIP BLUEPRINT AT A GLANCE

Name of Community/School: _____

Use this form to plan your leadership approach. You may fill in the names of existing programs (areas examined in your audit) under the grade levels they affect and add brief notes about planned changes. Include the names of programs you want to add, along with target dates for implementation. Use the "Notes" section at the bottom to list priority leadership characteristics, record your school leadership motto or definition, and any other general notes.

K	1	2	3	4	5	6

NOTES

CONTINUED»

From *Leadership Is a Life Skill* by Mariam G. MacGregor, M.S., copyright © 2018. This page may be reproduced for individual, classroom, or small group work only. For all other uses, contact Free Spirit Publishing Inc. at www.freespirit.com/permissions.

LEADERSHIP BLUEPRINT AT A GLANCE, continued

7	8	9	10	11	12

NOTES

From *Leadership Is a Life Skill* by Mariam G. MacGregor, M.S., copyright © 2018. This page may be reproduced for individual, classroom, or small group work only. For all other uses, contact Free Spirit Publishing Inc. at www.freespirit.com/permissions.

TWO

CREATING A CULTURE OF LEADERSHIP

CHAPTER 4
School Climate and Environment

Now that you've completed your audit and designed a Leadership Blueprint, momentum has likely started to build with stakeholders. If your blueprint includes making changes or additions to the school climate or environment, this chapter provides strategies to help you.

Preparing and Supporting Teachers as Leadership Change Agents

Initially, changing school climate falls on teachers. They set the tone in classrooms, in the halls, and throughout the campus with their behavior and attitude. There is a lot you can do to encourage teachers' leadership attitudes and actions.

Start by imagining the characteristics of someone you'd hire to focus on building leadership cultures—a change agent capable of driving the vision and goals of an organization to that common end goal, even when facing resistance. Change agents recognize that people might resist or struggle with changes unless they understand the why, what, and who details about the change, and most important in educational systems—*how a new initiative directly affects them*. Once you have a strong idea of the characteristics of this "new" person, work to create an atmosphere where those characteristics are encouraged and can thrive.

Now turn your eye to your current teaching staff. Some of your teachers probably possess some or all of the characteristics you seek. Others are ready, willing, and able to be coached to acquire them. Who on your staff is already positively affecting leadership cultures? Ask yourself or your students these two questions:

- Which of our teachers (and coaches, administrators, and so on) are successful at building leadership cultures during class times, co-curricular activities, and in the wider community?

- How can we replicate what those teachers are doing and inspire every teacher in our school or program to build leadership cultures for students?

Changing cultures to focus on leadership for all is exciting and challenging. Like anyone involved in a culture shift, teachers benefit from open conversations and relevant training. Give the staff in your school encouragement and strategies to:

- model leadership behavior

- give students choice in the classroom as much as possible

- recognize and reveal leadership qualities in students who may not be traditional leaders

- encourage a leadership atmosphere in which all students feel empowered to lead

- choose and develop student leaders that other students can respect

- establish teamwork, peer support, sportsmanship, and personal improvement as priorities over a winning-only philosophy

- work collaboratively with one another as a staff

Immersive, off-campus retreats are incredibly effective at getting people to dig deep on transforming into a leadership culture. Off-campus locations (even if only to a district training room or hotel conference ballroom) inspire new ways of looking at problems or opportunities. A kickoff retreat can be an inspiring way to pull together your staff prior to conducting your audit, while you analyze the audit, or when training for specific areas of your blueprint. Prior to scheduling, clearly communicate—in multiple ways and at multiple times—the purpose and goals of the retreat so teachers feel energized, not threatened or overwhelmed.

Whether you hold a retreat or conduct all your training on campus, provide professional development or in-service sessions for teachers to work together to revise curriculum. Provide multiple opportunities—planning periods, professional development days, summer prep time, and retreats—for teachers to work with instructional coaches to revise existing syllabi and lesson plans. Provide space—physical and mental—and time for teacher teams (by grade or subject area) to work together on aspects of the blueprint directly related to their work with students.

If possible, hire a professional facilitator or engage instructional coaches or others in your district who are skilled at bringing best ideas to fruition to lead group sessions. These sessions might even take the form of a district-wide mini-conference with breakout sessions and keynotes focused on different topics related to achieving leadership cultures.

Conducting intensives like retreats and professional development in-service days are more long-lasting when you also make time during each staff meeting to share successes, highlight opportunities, or address any concerns or unmet needs associated with this powerful culture shift.

Addressing Action Items Uncovered in Your Audit

In the audit you conducted in chapter 2, you may have addressed several areas related to school climate and environment:

- school mission statement or motto

- orientation programs for new students

- behavior modeled by adults

- handling conflict and complex issues

- school-wide celebrations, traditions, and expressions of school spirit

- condition and use of facilities and physical gathering places

These areas and others unique to your school or setting contain opportunities for creating high-impact changes that may be "easy wins" for your leadership culture. Here are some tips and strategies for making positive changes in each of these areas.

Creating a School Mission Statement or Motto

Establishing a shared, school-wide mission, definition, or vision of leadership is a way to reinforce the idea that teachers and students share a common set of beliefs and expectations on leadership and being leaders. It can be a complete sentence such as "Canandaigua City Schools strive for academic success for every child we serve and the development of good character in all students" or a simple phrase (or set of phrases) like the ones chosen by Vantage Point High School (see page 25).

With thousands of definitions of leadership floating around, it's tempting to develop a buzzword-filled phrase for the classroom or school. Instead, identify clear, simple, common leadership phrases associated with your school so the tone of your school environment feels relevant for everyone—staff, students, and parents.

Begin by asking staff and students to reflect on defining leadership personally *and* professionally. You can do this during a professional development day for teachers and then teachers can do it with students as a classroom assignment, writing prompt, or group discussion. Have students define leadership as it looks, feels, and sounds in the daily classroom experience to explore personal definitions of leaders and leadership.

You might use a platform like Poll Everywhere (in the App Store or at polleverywhere.com) and ask participants to log in online or through text message to a weeklong poll to help narrow down words and phrases. Start with broad questions, such as:

- What words describe our school?
- What words describe leadership to you?
- What does leadership look like at our school?
- What is your favorite leadership quote?

As the week progresses, look for common answers and themes from the results to narrow the scope of your questions. You might provide a list of phrases that came up often and ask students to choose three to five.

LEADERSHIP in ACTION

Mission and Vision Statements

Here are some examples of mission and vision statements to get you thinking.

- From T.M. Landry College Preparatory School (Breaux Bridge, LA): *The T.M. Landry mission is dedicated to promoting each child's self-worth and dignity in a supportive, educational, and safe environment while preparing them to prosper and flourish in a culturally diverse, technological society. T.M. Landry's goal is that every child not only gets into but gets THROUGH college.*

- From Lab Atlanta, a unique, immersive "city as classroom" semester experience for tenth graders across Atlanta: *We develop civically engaged, design-minded leaders focused on building a vibrant, sustainable future for themselves and the city of Atlanta.*

- From Hugh O'Brian Youth Leadership (HOBY), a global series of annual leadership conferences for sophomores, run locally and connected internationally: *To motivate and empower individuals to make a positive difference within our global society, through understanding and action, based on effective and compassionate leadership.*

No matter the method used, determine ahead of time how your ultimate choice will be made. Will your leadership advisory team put the final touches on your mission? Will students vote on three final recommendations? Will you send out a final poll listing options? You might have students (by classes or clubs) do a leadership mission statement video pitch—asking every teacher, regardless of subject area, to assign as a group project the creation of a school leadership mission statement. Then have the students and staff vote for their favorite. If you want your mission statement to be dynamic—changing from year to year—have students and staff select one winner to serve as your school's Annual

Leadership Theme for the year, and then repeat the same process at the same time every year.

Once you have a motto, find ways to broadcast it campus-wide (on your website, in newsletters, on scoreboards, and so on) to connect everyone in your school community to your dedication to leadership. It's easy to reinforce pro-social leadership behaviors and strengthen the message by working with teachers and students to implement activities such as:

- rotating students to conduct the morning announcements and asking them to finish with an inspirational quote connected to your mission or theme

- conducting poster contests promoting leadership ideas and motivating students to make a difference by promoting your school's mission or theme in the community

- asking students to create video PSAs using technology platforms (such as YouTube or iMovie) to show on your school website or on TV screens at your school

- assigning articles or a regular column on leadership topics to students in leadership or journalism classes for your school paper (or, if applicable, your community newspaper or magazine and Facebook pages or blogs)

- creating vinyl banners to hang in stairwells, entryways, the gym, athletic locker rooms, and other public spaces. Other signage and school-driven communication can reflect the same message throughout the year

New Student Orientation

Think about your current model. Typical orientations consist of school administrators or counselors passing out packets of paperwork and tentative class schedules, and plodding through a slide presentation for parents and kids in a large auditorium. Maybe you also provide a one-day "level-up" visit for students to spend a few hours at prospective middle or high schools. But orientation is an opportunity to do so much more.

Research demonstrates that when students feel connected to their new environment, greater academic success and social-emotional health follow. Colleges and universities work hard to provide a warm welcome to new students by emphasizing school culture and minimizing unknowns that might cause anxiety. Orientation may consist of multifaceted leadership retreats and teambuilding experiences that are engaging and focused on imparting the campus culture to new students. These are feasible changes that perpetuate a climate of leadership without requiring a large budget.

Student leaders can be extraordinary at delivering a positive first impression that introduces leadership as a school priority to new students and their parents. Consider creating an orientation team of staff and current students who can build a program that eases stress and helps new students quickly feel a part of your school. You will want to put in place a selection and training process for these current students, so they can deliver the consistent, inclusive, respectful message you want new students to receive. Like preparing teachers for their roles as change agents, consider conducting a daylong retreat for selected orientation leaders where they can build their own team and learn how to positively connect with and serve as leaders to younger students. Different roles for the orientation team may include training additional upper-grade students to serve as ambassadors who lead tours and answer questions for small groups of students.

The orientation experience can also include interactive, encouraging, two-way "pre-orientation" communications through an app like Remind (www.remind.com), or customizable apps like Guidebook (guidebook.com) and Legit Apps (www.legitapps.com), and through a dedicated page on your website that's monitored and updated by select student leaders. Messages can include encouraging notes, questions that might be typical of a nervous student (with an answer to follow), and important dates or reminders. If your school has a leadership theme for the year, provide T-shirts or other identifying swag to connect new students to the theme and each other. Offer two or three casual summer meet-and-greets for rising students (for grade-level changes or those new to the district) hosted by student leaders and school representatives.

Behavior Modeled by Adults

There's no magic here. If you want students to practice leadership skills and behaviors, make sure the adults in your schools do the same. Throughout this book you'll find ways to communicate this common message to staff, parents, and other adult stakeholders. For example, direct coaches to reinforce leadership by using positive leadership language with players, including speaking directly to students about "being encouragers, not discouragers" or "players on this team act like the leaders they want to follow." If your school commits to a leadership theme, remind the adults you lead that the theme applies to them as much as it applies to students.

Handling Conflict and Complex Issues

Teachers in every subject area benefit when there's an established standard of behavior. Classroom management is simplified in a leadership culture, because students begin self-regulating and expecting the same from peers.

Classroom management anchored in leadership helps students consistently practice soft skills. Encourage teachers to have students establish shared classroom values at the start of each school year or semester. At the middle and high school level, students in each class might even lead the discussion. These values are different from, but support, your school-wide leadership mission statement. They're the practical expectations set by each classroom for day-to-day success. It often takes less than twenty minutes during the first or second class of the year to establish these values. Provide adhesive newsprint and markers to create class posters. When posters are finished, laminate them so they last the entire school year. Or, provide already-laminated large sheets of newsprint that students and teachers can hang up and write on with dry-erase markers. Students can revise, update, or modify their classroom values throughout the year.

Here are some values and phrases I've seen on classroom (management) posters created by students and their teachers:

- Think before you speak in class, then offer a new idea. (Or: Raise your hand when you're ready to say something new instead of repeating what others say.)

- Model an "if not me, then who?" attitude. (For example, ask peers to stop doing something distracting, pick up a piece of trash when everyone else walks by, or encourage a peer who appears frustrated or disconnected.)

- Stand up when you see someone being bullied or treated unfairly.

- Listen to the teacher and to classmates.

- Be the boss of you, and let others be boss of themselves.
- Do the right thing, even when others aren't or seem to be pushing for something else.
- Work hard to do your best and champion others to do the same.
- Inspire each other in positive ways.
- Make good decisions.
- Be respectful to others and act respectable yourself.
- Resolve conflict in positive ways and seek help when it's needed.
- Do what's best for our class (or school) and expect others to do the same.

When students begin self-monitoring themselves and encouraging friends and classmates to "act like a leader" or "commit to leading," a natural shift occurs—away from focusing on who's causing problems to "how can we solve this problem together." Students then encourage positive peer behavior instead of pointing to others as "the problem." Students will have each other's backs because leadership is shaping the environment.

School-Wide Celebrations, Traditions, and Expressions of School Spirit

It's important to find ways for all students to feel proud of their school, express school spirit, and participate in celebrations and traditions. If your audit showed that certain student populations feel less membership in the school community than others, figure out why. Look at your celebrations and traditions to find ways to be more inclusive.

For example, maybe your school has a powerhouse basketball team that is often celebrated during pep rallies and assemblies. It's great to acknowledge the team's success, but deliberately find ways to talk up other teams and clubs as well, including academic and fine arts. Give student leaders a chance to speak about their groups during assemblies or morning announcements. You can host less conventional events such as a battle of the bands or poetry slam to engage and recognize kids who may not traditionally get that kind of attention from the school. Provide a suggestion box where students and faculty can suggest people who deserve to be recognized and feature them in the school newspaper or on the school website.

When collecting feedback from students and others, you may discover that the cultural weight of certain traditions, such as muffins with mom or donuts with dad, prom court, pep rallies, and senior sunrise, changes over time. Popular traditions may become outdated (like hazing) or exclusionary (like clubs restricted based on gender, physical ability, or other characteristics). When you see that happening, it's time to help students (and adults—especially alumni or parents from your school) make *new* traditions by trying things that challenge existing traditions.

Condition and Use of Facilities and Physical Gathering Places

You don't need to rebuild your gym if it's far from state of the art. When it comes to facilities, the goal is to do what you can to promote a sense of pride for everyone who uses or sees the space. Your audit may have revealed that the cafeteria is excessively messy after meal times or outside areas of your school need beautification. Often, people forget that physical spaces are reflections of the people inside—and the people inside can do a lot to improve things. Graffiti or trash elimination can be addressed by student clubs or student government. Students can paint murals that support your leadership theme on plain cinderblock walls. "Senior Tiles" are popular traditions that strengthen leadership culture by asking seniors to paint a standard ceiling tile with their favorite inspirational quote or memorable moment at school.

I know of school programs in old or minimalist buildings, serving highly transient communities, that are neat and tidy because students are nurtured as leaders, no matter how few or many days they attend. Your school can have quarterly shared cleanup days instead of using trash pickup to punish kids in detention. Sides of old buildings can become climbing walls. Students or clubs can sell spirit T-shirts (improve school spirit) to fundraise for device-charging stations in classrooms (improve facilities). If your facilities are a major hindrance to building pride and a leadership climate, you may find support from the 21st Century School Fund (21csf.org).

Consider Outside Resources

There are a lot of creative approaches to helping leadership flourish in your school climate, and it's easy to feel overwhelmed. You don't have to make changes to everything covered in this chapter; every school is unique, and it's important to identify the changes that will make the greatest difference in your situation.

It's also true that you don't have to do everything on your own. School districts and communities all over have designed or implemented preexisting programs to strengthen their leadership climate. You can use resources like these to kick-start changes in your school environment. For example, Ben's Bells, a community organization in Tucson, Arizona, changes school environments by teaching the practice of intentional kindness and empathy. Their staff regularly visits schools throughout the region delivering their message. Teachers, students, and parents consider Ben's Bells part of the fabric of Tucson—true evidence of a changed climate. The organization is creating a widespread culture of leadership by turning the kindness message into a leadership practice through the Ben's Bells Step Up! program. It trains and informs students on how to serve as peer leaders for those struggling with personal or emotional challenges.

It can be well worth your time to research resources like this in your area. While the initial goal behind implementing a program like Ben's Bells at your school might be changing your school climate, you may also find that it sets you up to implement other leadership improvements in academic content, student clubs, and opportunities for student-driven leadership.

LEADERSHIP in ACTION

Hard Questions Lead to Hard-Won Changes

Fernando Branch, assistant principal at Denver's Noel Community Arts School, is a leadership school climate change agent with a reputation for being a school turnaround expert. He understands what it takes to infuse leadership cultures in settings that feel toxic or chaotic, both from the student and staff perspective. He also understands that change happens slowly, it can result in staff attrition, and it most definitely involves difficult conversations.

In 2017, his student population was 60 percent Latino, 20 percent black, and 10 percent other races, with possibly 25

percent of the students pursuing post-secondary education. The low percentage of students going to college
or pursuing vocations after graduation didn't square with
the school's motto, "Artists, Activists, Innovators." When
Branch was hired, though, he saw that the school experience was being driven by adults who expected little from
students in terms of embodying these qualities. To address
this, some teachers were asked to reapply for their jobs or
move on. Absenteeism rates were high and continuation
rates from middle to high school were low. He advocated
for the district to reassign grades kindergarten through fifth
into neighborhood elementary schools so more attention
and resources could be focused on grades sixth through
twelfth, where students were beginning to perform better.

When Branch started at the school, he embraced his
role to model distributive leadership. Instead of being "the
person in charge," he sought to put "the system in charge,"
communicating (in person, in writing) to students and staff
that every member of Noel's community was expected
to take ownership for the good and bad. To Branch, "the
system" meant the school community, which was a new
way of thinking for kids and parents who typically viewed
the system as rules and roadblocks imposed by others.

To start building a school climate where everyone
is expected to be a leader, Branch set standards on
attendance (consequences if absences exceed a certain number), grade requirements for earning credit (no
automatic leveling up), and consistent professionalism by
teachers (even if frustrated). He coaches staff members on
professionalism instead of waiting until annual performance
reviews. He wears suits and ties (or bowties) as a visual
symbol of his own professionalism. His Bowtie Tuesday
Club inspires students to dress up and wear bowties or
bows too. Another obvious change to the school climate
and environment is his physical presence: Every day he
walks the halls to have conversations, build relationships,
and reinforce a school-wide culture of ownership, good
character, and integrity.

Most of all, he asked hard questions and made tough changes:

- "When our AP test scores average 0.7, why are we still putting resources here?" (Despite angry protests, he temporarily removed some AP classes from the course list and moved resources elsewhere.)

- "If our student government selects students based only on GPA (3.5 or above), only 5 percent of our school is eligible to participate. Why is that our benchmark?" (He eliminated the GPA requirement, instituted a self-selection and election process, and opened candidacy to students in any grade. Leadership selection ideas like these are further explored in chapter 6.)

- "If we want students to engage in accountability talk, why are they not joining us at the table to discuss school-related functions (operations, process, programming, satisfaction)?" (Students now complete a student satisfaction survey and are involved in every operational process at the school.)

- "We ask parents, teachers, and community members to be engaged in our school, so why aren't we transparent about the results we want to achieve with students, now and in the future?" (He moved the school's graduation ceremony to the largest performing arts complex in Denver, providing a vivid reality of the possible futures for diverse students attending an arts school.)

For a while, these questions and changes caused others to perceive him as an enemy, not an advocate. To overcome resistance, he relied on his personal leadership talents: He was generous in expressing his belief in the talents of others—staff and students, including those doubtful of change. He sought to build warm, authentic relationships through small, casual conversations. He modeled transparency and leadership-driven engagement techniques he expected between staff and students—also expecting students to act respectfully to teachers. He also communicated honestly—good news or bad—with parents. All this helped establish a climate of "we're in this together."

For the 2017–2018 school year, Noel Community Arts School recruited its largest class of ninth graders in years. It's a good sign, but Branch knows change doesn't happen overnight; he remains patient in the process, because he's confident that a leadership culture soon will be the school's normal.

Branch recognizes that when he walks into the school, and when students, teachers, and parents walk into the school, "Everyone shares the same magic dust"— meaning everyone has access to the same opportunities at the school if they each understand *why* they're doing what they're doing through shared leadership and ownership of the school.

Though he's early in his tenure at this school, he is well-positioned for success because of his relatable leadership skills. You may be the Branch at your school or district. If so, your personality and commitment to building leadership cultures is the greatest asset at your disposal! And you probably have one or more leaders like Branch on your staff, eager to have their voices heard and ideas noticed. Keep bringing people together to keep your momentum going!

If you want to know more, here's an article highlighting his leadership approach and commitment to building a leadership environment and school climate: bit.ly/2o HaeWq. Or do an internet search for "Fernando Branch."

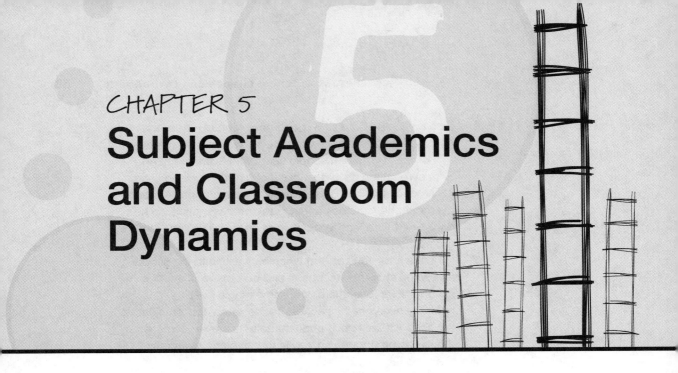

CHAPTER 5
Subject Academics and Classroom Dynamics

Integrating leadership across the curriculum means "tagging" student learning with leadership throughout the K–12 experience. Incorporating leadership into academics creates consistency in exposing students to the wide range of positive possibilities associated with being a leader and understanding leadership in practical ways. It also exposes kids who face barriers to being involved with co-curricular activities or teens who have jobs, so they're not excluded from developing leadership and soft skills.

Work closely with your teachers to identify the specific leadership skills and knowledge you want every student to learn and demonstrate at school and beyond. The list of leadership skills on pages 19–22 is a great starting point for discussing with your staff but attempting to teach every concept or skill on the list is unrealistic.

Ideally, strive to expose every student in every grade to leadership lessons or experiences in the academic classroom every semester. In primary and intermediate grades, this might happen through several assignments on different topics, while middle and high school could get this exposure through one class (not necessarily a designated leadership course).

Apply the 70-20-10 Rule

The 70-20-10 rule was developed after thirty years of research by the international leadership consulting firm Center for Creative Leadership. The rule refers to the ratio of types of experiences that lead to people's most effective learning: 70 percent challenging assignments, 20 percent developmental relationships, and 10 percent course work and training. It has become a popular formula in the workplace. For example, Google uses it as a way for employees to manage their career road maps—dedicating 70 percent of their time to their primary responsibilities (what they're hired to do), 20 percent to working with others on related projects, and 10 percent to learning new skills through formal learning or a side project. The rule is used in many companies to focus employee training and development: 70 percent of learning comes from on-the-job application, 20 percent is gained informally through networking and mentors, and 10 percent comes from formal training sessions.

Applying this concept to how all subjects are taught, this translates to students spending:

- 70 percent of their time learning through independent study and curious inquiry
- 20 percent of their time working on projects with others
- 10 percent of their time learning from direct instruction

Applying this rule can help shape your approach to leadership across the curriculum. The largest portion of learning (70 percent) occurs "on the job," through homework assignments, independent reading, watching films, and interactive experiences such as project-based learning in the classroom, but also football games, fine arts, student clubs, service projects, and grade-level outdoor labs and trips (like school visits to tour Washington, D.C.). The second-largest portion (20 percent) comes from working directly with others through group or partner homework projects and classroom discussions. And the smallest portion of learning, just 10 percent, is devoted to formal teaching in a class, at a workshop, or online. I'm not suggesting that during fifty-minute sessions you're only teaching for ten minutes. Rather, for the overall learning experience over the course of a semester, 10 percent of what students learn comes from direct instruction.

A number of elementary, middle, and high schools in districts throughout Colorado integrate leadership across the curriculum using the 70-20-10 rule. Time spent in and out of class is multipurposed between instruction (10), hands-on learning through mentoring or projects (20), and important organic interactions (70). Third-grade English language arts classes prepare third graders to serve as book buddies and allocate weekly times for third graders to read to and be read to by kindergartners. Fifth-grade course work integrates science, math, and leadership and team skills in preparation for students attending Outdoor Lab, a week in the mountains focused on environmental science while working together on meals, projects, and learning leadership skills. Schools host annual fun runs, and classes focus on healthy lifestyles, physical fitness, and nutrition, as well as teamwork and respect in preparation for the entire school (plus teachers, administrators, parents, and community members) to run through the town while supporting and cheering each other on. At the high school level, fun runs are planned, promoted, and executed by students and include a fundraising element for their student leadership activities or classes.

Addressing Action Items Uncovered in Your Audit

In the audit you conducted in chapter 2, you may have addressed several areas related to academics and classroom dynamics:

- In what ways are students given ownership over learning?

- How can we structure assignments so that students use leadership skills? What alternate grading methods can we incorporate that recognize leadership behaviors and application?

- Where can leadership content easily be integrated (in certain lessons, subjects, or classes such as advisory)?

- When current events that reflect on leadership in the real world occur, are teachers given the latitude to include timely discussions of or new content related to that leadership moment? Which teachers do this well and how can their ideas be applied to other classes?

These areas and others unique to your school or setting contain opportunities for creating high-impact changes that reflect those "quick wins" for your leadership culture mentioned in chapter 3. Here are some tips and strategies for making positive changes in each of these areas.

Giving Students Ownership of Learning

Offer opportunities to act. Establish unique ways for all students in grades K–12 to take action and be involved in formal and informal leadership roles in the classroom, programs, and other experiences. Students have interest areas and passions beyond the classroom that they're eager to showcase. Consider asking students to fill out an interest survey early in the school year; teachers can find ways to have students create lesson plans when their hobbies and class content connect. For example, if some students love building with Legos, teachers can ask students to help design and teach a geometry lesson that combines teamwork and Legos. If students volunteer at pet shelters, ask them to research and initiate a program like SitStayRead in the Chicago area (www .sitstayread.org) or Reading Education Assistance Dogs (www.therapyanimals .org) where children read to therapy animals.

Make learning real. There are plenty of ways to expand leadership in academics by moving beyond textbooks. Ask students to role-play concepts with one another to explain a topic to the entire class. When something occurs in real life that aligns with a textbook lesson, ask students to reframe the lesson by drawing analogies and conclusions from what they're observing or experiencing instead of from the pages of a book. Films and popular TV shows are another way to make learning real. Teacher can ask, "Imagine you're [name of character]—what would you do in that situation?"

Put students in roles where they can serve as peer coaches and mentors. Establish a process that prepares and supports older students to serve as leadership role models and mentors for younger or less-experienced students. One way to do this is to have students learn how to be leadership coaches to their peers. Coaches provide feedback designed to guide people to improve their skills. Peer coaches focus on helping others get better at a specific task—learning better time management skills, building better communication skills, or mastering a difficult skill in a talent area such as music, art, theater, or athletics.

Whereas mentors serve as advisors and sounding boards because they've experienced what younger kids are experiencing, peer coaches can be taught to step back from the situation and observe what's going on, then provide their peers with specific tips and techniques. Peer coaches also remind students that improvement requires practice, an important concept to learn at any age.

Structuring Assignments and Grading Methods to Incorporate Leadership Skills

For teachers who are apprehensive about overhauling lesson plans, or for classes such as AP courses where the curriculum is mostly set, help teachers design assignment formats that involve group work so students learn to use leadership and soft skills without changing the content being taught. That way students are learning leadership skills even if they aren't explicitly studying leadership. Here are some ideas.

Have students work in groups. When students work together, they have to use leadership skills such as teamwork and communication. They have to negotiate roles and decisions about content, and all students have opportunities to take on the role of leader within the group. Kids and teens enjoy working together to solve social problems, achieve academic goals, and imagine the future. Working together leads to a greater sensitivity to the needs of others.

Have students present to the class. Today's students can discern a good presentation from a bad one, and educators often use top-notch TED talks or well-crafted YouTube videos when teaching. But *seeing* a good presentation is very different from *executing* one. Opportunities to present lessons or "stand and deliver" the results of research and team projects in front of classmates teaches students valuable skills. Consider recording student presentations to discuss privately with the presenters, or have peers provide written evaluations of the visuals, organization of content, use of gestures, and confidence of a presenter. All students will develop a stronger sense of empathy for other presenters as they gain firsthand knowledge presenting and critiquing presentations.

Student Choice

When employing strategies to give students ownership of their learning, instead of structuring assignments as individual endeavors, consider this creative method used by a middle school Spanish I teacher in Texas. At the start of each semester, she hands out a list of the content units she'll cover and various ways she intends to measure learning. She embraces educational technology, having students complete Duolingo for individual ongoing review, and integrating group dynamics using competitive quizzes on Quizlet. Leadership culture comes from the student choice technique she uses to organize assignments. There are eight projects throughout the school year, and each project can be completed using a different *format* (three formats can be repeated): video, paper, stand-up demonstration, poster (presented to group), or foldout booklet (walk-around gallery); and using a different *method*: individual, partner, trio, or small group. If students want to use the same format twice, they must use one of the other formats before doing so. Once students have used the same method twice, they can't use it again. Students learn firsthand how to prioritize, manage time, set goals, and think creatively. Public speaking skills are enhanced because many of the assignments require a presentation. Students complete peer evaluations for the three methods that require working together. They also learn how to address conflicts and consult with the teacher when things go poorly.

Adjust rubrics. If teachers evaluate student work and projects using a rubric, ask departments to create a section in their rubrics to directly measure leadership—whether demonstrated through knowledge or behavior. You might dedicate an in-service professional development session to creating your school's rubrics.

Be confident that your teachers already have some interesting methods that they're using and create a way for teachers to share their methods with one another. Maybe they're incorporating and recording interviews with town leaders or engaging in debates as an alternative to written essays. Maybe they're using storyboards like advertising agencies to explain sequences of information and ideas. In band or orchestra classes, teachers might be evaluating leadership by asking students to write bars of music or lyrics (alone or in a team) and play their own compositions in front of peers once a semester.

Edutopia (edutopia.org) has an archive of creative ideas for measuring learning at all grade levels, many of these ideas can be applied to teaching leadership. Additional methods for designing and measuring leadership learning for older students can be developed collaboratively with your team. Recognizing that students have different learning modalities and techniques by which they demonstrate their learning in other classes can guide you when you start to design tools to measure students' leadership growth.

Integrating Leadership Content Into Subjects and Classes

It's not necessary for every lesson and every class to focus on leadership. Instead, support teachers to introduce or align leadership in ways that enhance their core subject matter or areas of expertise. For example, writing prompts related to leadership topics can be selected in language arts, or writing styles (like letter writing, persuasive essays, and so on) can be taught by asking students to address a larger societal issue. Social studies and history classes have plenty of natural openings for leadership lessons—evaluating great speeches, understanding leaders throughout history (positive and negative), and the impact of history itself on what we expect of leaders. Leadership lessons on effective communication and teambuilding can be incorporated into elective classes classified as "Partner PE" or "Partner Art," where typically developing kids and kids with special needs are paired together to learn subject content. Speech and debate classes provide opportunities for leadership lessons on ethics and integrity (learning to research and argue a position with which you may not agree) and how to engage active listening skills (listening to understand). Math concepts can be taught with practical applications like using real-life leadership examples in word problems and teaching mathematical problem-solving techniques in group settings to promote communication, consensus, and negotiation skills.

There is a collection of sample leadership lessons on pages 144–148 to guide you on aligning leadership with subject areas like mathematics, physics, writing, and communication (speech).

Incorporating Appropriate Current Events Into Instruction Time

In subject areas where leadership is easy to integrate, such as English language arts, history, advisory, service learning, government, social sciences, speech, and journalism, teachers should be encouraged to incorporate current events and real-world situations for timely discussions or new content related to that leadership moment. Here are some ideas:

- a five-minute "news flash" moment at the start of class during which small groups of students read an article and identify three or four leadership issues

- in a primary class, students learn a leadership-word-of-the-day related to something happening in the local community; teachers lead a discussion about the word's meaning, its importance, and how it is reflected in the current event

- students evaluate election results from local, national, and international elections to determine voting percentages and rations compared to a country's population

- students watch or listen to a TV or radio news program designed for or run by students (such as CNN Student News, Youth Radio, or Planet Money) and discuss as a class what stood out the most to students

A Few More Ideas

Leadership cultures thrive when students become accustomed to leadership experiences and activities inside and outside their classrooms. Schools achieve this by intentionally connecting active learning with leadership-focused content in many subject areas. Here are a few more ways to connect leadership and academic content:

- Encourage staff to use leadership vocabulary and references regardless of subject area.

- Format middle and high school leadership classes as academic offerings (in many schools, they're classified as a general elective or a social studies elective) instead of focusing on planning social events and spirit activities; allow enrollment based on both self-selection and recommendation by peers or teachers. See pages 110–112 for more about leadership classes.

- Implement a leadership book club consisting of novels with characters who demonstrate leadership qualities, biographies/autobiographies of leaders, or books about leadership topics; identify monthly or semester titles that are either already being taught in the curriculum or that can be accessed in the school library; organize additional events (brown-bag lunches, movies, speakers, field trips, and so on) around the book.

- Maintain a leadership library—a collection of leadership-themed books (fiction, nonfiction, biographies, novels with main characters who demonstrate leadership traits, books on using leadership characteristics) in the school library or in another easily accessed area.

- Establish peer tutoring programs—selecting and preparing a team of subject-matter-expert peers who have specific tutoring hours during advisory and before and after school.

- Create student study partner programs (reading partners, tech aides, summer bridge).

- Organize a leadership speaker and film series aligned with subject matter; piggyback classroom and school visits by authors, athletes, local and national influencers, and others already scheduled for community events or visits (partner with your local library, university, businesses, chamber of commerce, mayor's office, performing arts, and so on).

When the thread of leadership runs through all subjects, everyone receives the same message and shares the same expectations. There's power in this alone. Beyond that, classroom management becomes easier, because student learning is anchored in these shared expectations. Troublesome behavior becomes an outlier as positive social norms take over. And, as students work together, academic subject matter and leadership concepts connect directly to their success beyond graduation.

CHAPTER 6
Teams, Clubs, and Student-Driven Leadership

Students have many opportunities to get involved with their school outside the classroom, and co-curricular activities can be key to achieving personal fulfillment as well as creating an inclusive, leadership-rich campus culture. Besides building skills and gaining experience in the subject of their team or club, students get a lot out of being involved in after-school activities—camaraderie, teamwork, experience managing differences, experience setting and achieving goals, fun, and opportunities to lead. If your school has limited offerings, find ways to offer something for everyone who wants to be involved. This chapter provides multiple suggestions for doing that as well as for improving engagement and effectiveness.

LEADERSHIP in ACTION

All for Clubs and Clubs for All

Sharron Jackson, principal of O.W. Holmes Middle School in Dallas, Texas, launched a diverse, multi-club program that engages every student—more than 800—at a school where typically only 10 to 15 percent of the students participated in after-school activities (mostly athletics). She named the new program the T.R. Lee Leadership Academy, after the principal of the middle school when Jackson attended.

The forty-plus clubs, all meeting on the last Friday of every month, do more than bring kids together around a common interest. Students are required to get involved in any club in which they're also expected to take an active leadership role, plan a service project together, and learn "successful habits" (leadership lessons) during each meeting. Each club elects its own leaders who, with the help of an advisor (a teacher or community volunteer), guide the group in designing their service project, lead discussions on different topics, and ensure success. As a result, Jackson and her staff have successfully created a leadership culture that engages teachers and community volunteers as mentors and gets students thinking about leadership regardless of what club they join.

Preparing and Supporting Coaches and Activity Advisors as Leadership Change Agents

Teachers and staff who lead athletic teams, arts clubs, academic clubs, student government, other student-driven leadership programs, and other extra-curricular activities have great opportunities to establish and reinforce the leadership culture at your school—and they also have greater responsibility to do so. Their interactions with students outside class may be more personal and more intense than classroom relationships. Students may look up to them more than they do other teachers, and these teachers will often have more influence on the students they work with.

There will be overlap between your teacher training efforts and the training you provide to coaches and activity advisors, because most serving in these roles are teachers. This subset of staff is responsible for chaperoning off-campus events (for example, as the visiting team at away games, at academic competitions, and volunteering in the community), and so will benefit from at least one in-service session focused on code of conduct and reflecting your leadership culture expectations off campus. Encourage these adult leaders to spend extra time training student leaders on how to behave at off-campus competitions and events.

You will also want to provide these coaches and advisors with ideas and resources for bringing together their student leadership throughout the school year—for example, by designing a monthly (or biweekly, depending on season length) Captain's Roundtable for all athletic team captains or Student Leadership Roundtable for club and activity leaders. Depending on how band, orchestra, choir, and theater function in your school, these teachers or advisors may want to put together their own Fine Arts Student Leadership Roundtable. In all cases, a roundtable is a way to bring together students and their advisors to discuss ideas, challenges, successes, and other topics important to successfully leading a student group. Each roundtable meets separately, and when they do, every athletic team (male and female) or individual club has a representative at the respective roundtable. Most often it's the captain or president, but I've occasionally seen students chosen to represent a group because of their leadership skills.

To ensure coaches and advisors feel confident with being school-climate influencers, provide plenty of opportunities to communicate about the role of clubs, teams, and other student organizations in the school environment. It can be useful to schedule quarterly meetings with advisors and coaches to discuss leadership as it relates to their advising roles. The additional time commitment this group gives to student organizations requires time from you to make sure concerns are heard and they have an outlet to share ideas and engage with others sharing the same roles. These quarterly meetings also allow space for people to share ideas, get support, and hear successes from others.

Effective Advising Increases Student Ownership

Advisors who work with student leaders as partners, serving as thoughtful sounding boards instead of as their directors, can make a memorable impact. When student leaders have advisors teaching them *how* to lead better, they gain greater ownership of the success of their teams and organizations. Hearing coaches or advisors say, "You need to delegate better" isn't helpful. Hearing "How can I help you learn to delegate better?" is. The challenge is to prepare advisors to provide less prescriptive guidance and more dedicated mentoring with the student leaders.

Encourage students to take "ownership" of their group and be conscientious about using that word. The people whose profiles and stories are shared in this book used it frequently. When there's a lack of ownership, clubs and teams fail or members feel disconnected. When people *take* ownership, outcomes are affected positively: Kids who have positive or high-performing experiences on sports teams or in other groups often share this in common—they usually say their team's or club's success came from every player or member taking ownership, whether they won or lost.

Student leaders want their voices valued. Unfortunately, it's not uncommon for teachers and administrators to discount their views, judge the way they lead their club or team, or express disapproval without assistance. Even worse are advisors and coaches who belittle, shame, or use sarcasm as methods to "inspire" young leaders. If students describe advisors or coaches at your school this way (or you know firsthand of teachers and coaches like this), the initial introduction to a leadership culture may feel fake and inauthentic to students. If your district or school has a history of discounting student voices, student leaders will view you through a cautious and potentially distrustful lens. Even in these environments, kids and teens can start to feel empowered and excited about the good that's happening over time. Do your best to coach advisors and coaches to lead with positivity and encouragement, even when students make mistakes, so that those student leaders will remain engaged.

Sharing Power

On the micro-level of a school, the principal typically possesses school-wide power, teachers possess the primary power in their classrooms, and students possess social power among peers. Some teachers struggle with "giving up" power in their classrooms or school because they feel that giving it up means kids will create chaos! In my experience, both in the classroom and when training teens for leadership responsibilities, transferring power to students has shown me that students will wisely use their power and self-monitor each other to prevent chaos.

Balancing power means students are provided *legitimate* opportunities, not token titles or shallow experiences, and they are expected to take on significant responsibilities. Confident educators master this process by learning how to maintain professional distance in exchange for promoting appropriate self-actualizing and autonomy of students. Some ways to do this include:

- working with students on preplanning meetings, events, or other programming
- having students create lists of pros and cons when teams, clubs, or organizations are making decisions or choices regarding activities and other programming associated with their group
- controlling prescriptive tendencies (telling students what they should and shouldn't do)
- serving as a consultant as students work through large-scale school or community service projects

While failure and mistakes may occur, coaches and advisors in leadership cultures seize these opportunities to refine leadership learning rather than responding punitively.

Kids and teens have access to an incredible amount of information through the internet (podcasts, independently released music, YouTube) and in real life (missions and service projects, outdoor immersion experiences and internships, international travel, and in-the-street survival). This easy access to information and firsthand experiences equip them with plenty of interesting ideas and resources that will help them when they share responsibility for co-curricular leadership activities at your school. They're likely comfortable researching online to find creative ideas to try with team members, re-creating a leadership activity they learned at camp or a job, or using social media to get people excited about club activities and events.

Addressing Action Items Uncovered in Your Audit: Teams and Clubs

"Teams and clubs" covers a wide range of student organizations. Teams include sanctioned competitive sports as well as intramural and casual sports events organized through school. Clubs often are started due to requests by students, with faculty sponsors actively guiding the direction of the organization. These student clubs and organizations frequently include a wide range of competitive and noncompetitive groups that revolve around service (Care Club, Interact, Key Club), academics (Academic Decathlon, math club, debate), theater and fine arts (improv team, art, ceramics, slam poetry), intramural sports (single gender and coed ultimate Frisbee, flag football, 5k running, dodgeball, fishing, Newcomb ball, mountain biking), and unique interests (faith groups, Quidditch, coding, cooking, Legos, card games, TED talks, speaking club, Minecraft).

The culture of a club or sports team can change over time. If a group is perceived negatively by students but positively by adults, it can create a leadership credibility problem that needs fixing. If the problem stems from poor coaching, then work directly with the coaches to fix it—hold them accountable for allowing (or turning a blind eye) to bad behavior. If the problem stems from the student culture, you'll need to work closely with students to fix it. Or maybe there's no problem, and you've simply identified teams and clubs as an area where leadership culture can be improved. Regardless of your situation, the audit questions on pages 28–30 suggest some areas where you can start to make improvements.

Help coaches and advisors prepare student leaders beyond the leadership learning they're gaining in other school areas by identifying ways students can lead in their teams and clubs. Here are some ideas.

Choosing Student Leaders

Find ways to allow students to self-select for leadership opportunities (rather than relying on votes, nominations, or other selection processes). For example, invite interested students to apply or write a brief essay responding to a club-related question or an explanation about why they want to be involved or chosen to participate. Have student leaders host an info session or panel representing the team or organization and allow anyone who attends to join.

Maintain selectivity for leadership experiences where it's relevant and necessary for success (honor societies, ability-based sports teams, advisory boards, and so on); if an organization's value springs from membership or selection standards, keep those in place.

Allowing Student Leaders to Make Meaningful Decisions

Allow student leaders to make decisions that truly affect the organization—decisions that show they are trusted and their opinions are valued. Ask students to conduct an abbreviated audit about what in their organization is going well and what's not. If team members aren't upholding leadership standards, serve as a consultant for student leaders to decide what to do with the members.

Provide choices so that student leaders can apply newly gained skills and knowledge. These kinds of choices might include how and when to select new leaders, when to schedule events, what it takes to be considered an active member, and what competitions to participate in. For example, in Texas, some academic, music, extracurricular, and all sports teams are governed by the University Interscholastic League (UIL). Aside from athletics, students or their teams can choose to participate in as many or as few of the competitions as they want.

Developing Leadership Skills

Require coaches and advisors to make leadership skills and training an implicit part of the team or club experience. Provide consistent training on important topics such as running effective meetings, communicating difficult decisions, inclusion, and collaboration. Consistency can be achieved by spending fifteen minutes at the start or end of a group meeting or conducting thirty- to forty-five-minute leadership sessions every other time the group meets. For example, when I trained youth volunteers for a nonprofit, the students volunteered for three hours at a time. Following their volunteer time, they participated together in a leadership session aligned with the mission of the nonprofit and the kids they served by being volunteers. Leadership training does not need to be rigid or overtly obvious. Adults can help student leaders build skills in a variety of ways, such as:

- encouraging student leaders to present to their peers and be prepared to answer questions

- communicating to team or club members the expectation that members listen to their fellow students before asking questions or putting down ideas

- providing guidance and learning opportunities when a student leader makes a mistake (or fails and wants to quit)

- protecting the health and safety of all students associated with the organization, including stepping in when student leaders may be unaware of potentially damaging consequences

The more opportunities student leaders get to engage in public speaking, run meetings, delegate tasks, and build their teams, the more they learn to manage their positional power with an audience, strengthen their communication and critical thinking skills, and learn to adapt to various situations.

Of course, adult leaders can also conduct topical sessions with their teams and clubs to more explicitly address leadership. For example, if you're working with a middle school club that's just getting to know each other, coordinate with student leaders to facilitate a low-risk communication activity like "Salt and Pepper" below.

LEADERSHIP in ACTION

Salt and Pepper

Materials needed: Quarter sheets of paper or index cards, tape, writing utensils

Time required: 20–25 minutes depending on the size of the group.

Group size: 6–40 (best with even number of participants)

Prior to the activity, think of obvious things that go together in pairs, for example, salt and pepper. Write one item from each pair on a sheet of paper, so that every sheet has a match to make a pair. Make as many sheets as there are group members (but they should all be different pairs). Or, if time allows, have each person in the group brainstorm a pair and, without sharing their pair with others, write the items on two sheets. Collect the sheets and proceed with the rest of the activity.

At the beginning of the activity, tape one sheet on the back of each participant without letting him or her see what is on the sheet. On your "go" signal, participants walk around asking only yes or no questions of one another to figure out what is written on their sheet and who is their matching partner. Once participants successfully find their partner, they must sit down and interview each other, finding out three to five interesting facts about each partner.

Possible pairs: Salt and pepper, ketchup and mustard, Mickey Mouse and Minnie Mouse, right and left, Romeo and Juliet, Batman and Robin, coffee and tea, bread and butter, milk and cookies, Harry Potter and Ron Weasley, peas and carrots, cocoa and marshmallows, burgers and fries, chips and salsa, baseball and bat

Variations:

- Choose pairs that are the names of diverse local or national leaders from history or modern times.

- Write specific interview questions on the backside of each quarter sheet before placing them on participants' backs.

- Have pairs introduce their partners to the rest of the group, sharing what they learned about them.

- If time is running short, instead of doing short interviews right then, tell participants they must eat lunch together to get to know each other better. You can give them a list of questions or a short survey they answer together during lunch.

Addressing Action Items Uncovered in Your Audit: Student-Driven Leadership

Young people are natural helpers, wired from childhood to respond with compassion and care for others. Serving as leaders with peers continues to build their empathy muscles. As adults, we sometimes focus so much on running the show that we forget this. Student-driven leadership generally refers to programs initiated by students because they see a need or because someone (an adult or students) realize students will make a greater impact than adults doing or saying the same thing. A tremendous amount of student-driven leadership takes the shape of older students connecting with or serving peers and younger students. Here are some ideas.

Student athlete outreach. Younger students often consider athletes local heroes. Consider implementing a program for high school athletes to visit elementary and middle schools to talk about the importance of education, giving back to the community, and staying focused on success. For an example of how this might look, read about the student athletes at Texas Christian University who started the SPARK (Strong Players Are Reaching Kids) program (bit.ly /2FV2MDJ). It would be your high school athletes partnering with middle and elementary students, but if your district has a close relationship with a local college or university, you might consider asking them so that high school athletes also benefit from older mentors and role models.

Student assistants or teacher aides (middle or high school). In many middle and high schools, students can earn elective credit by serving as a teacher's assistant or as student assistants. And in many cases, they're underutilized! For teacher aides, be intentional about putting students in classes that capitalize on their strengths (for example, a strong writer serving as a teacher aide in journalism or writing classes) so they can take an active role helping peers or serving as a tutor during the class they're assigned. Student assistants, say in the counseling office, can help co-lead friendship groups or be trained to assist and guide students who come with questions rather than simply delivering passes or sitting around.

Teacher cadets. If your traditional or career-tech program offers a teacher education training program, coordinate with fellow administrators to place each of these students with mentoring teachers throughout district classrooms.

Middle-to-high-school-transition teams and ninth-grade ambassadors. Partner upper-class students with small groups of rising ninth graders to ease the transition to high school. Ambassadors can meet with the transitioning students in the spring of their eighth-grade year, host a walk-around tour and Q & A session at the high school during the summer, and then be scheduled to greet their small groups on the first day of school. Ambassadors can also be positioned around the cafeteria during the first several weeks of each semester, paying attention to new students who are eating alone or having a hard time navigating new routines.

Girls or boys leadership mentors or mixed-gender social-skills mentoring groups. Mentoring groups can be very effective at providing a safe space for kids of all ages to discuss issues. Select and train students (peers and older) to help run these groups and serve as 1:1 partners with boys or girls who may be struggling with making friends, socializing, or navigating school. Be sure to have your school counselor or AVID professional involved as well, in case things get too personal. There are a variety of resources to help you design a program like this including Girls Inc. (girlsinc.org/what-we-do), Boys To Men (boystomen.org), the state of Georgia's Leading Ladies of Legacy (leadingladie soflegacy.org), and your local Boys and Girls Clubs.

Principal's advisory council. Assemble students from all grades and different interest areas to meet regularly to discuss and problem-solve school-related issues such as vandalism and cheating. The council can also talk about handling difficult problems your school may be experiencing like suicide, bullying, and hate crimes. These students can provide valuable perspectives on these issues.

Peer tutors. Select and train students with strong academic skills in any subject. Have them hold regular tutoring hours in the sponsoring teacher's room after school or during lunch or advisory periods in the school day.

Peer helpers/mediators. Train students to help with conflict mediation and strengthening appropriate responses to conflict and stress, because fellow students can be exceptionally successful at de-escalating situations without adults getting involved. This approach is used so widely that a quick internet search of "peer mediation K–12" can provide a variety of models on which to base your program.

Honor Society team helpers. Engage students in your National Honor Society (NHS) or National Junior Honor Society (NJHS) to help with academically related competitions such as geography bee, spelling bee, and battle of books. Both NJHS and NHS have community service requirements to maintain membership, and because many of the academic clubs meet after school, you can partner honors students with teachers to join them during the group's practice times.

Activity monitors and playground partners. High school leaders such as student council members, Key Club or other volunteer organization members, and athletes are great resources for elementary and middle school field days, fundraising carnivals, or similar school-wide events. Little kids look up to older students, and teachers will love having teen leaders around to corral and cheer on the younger students. You might also implement an elective credit Community Service class that requires consistent volunteer hours from students taking the class to serve as playground partners (serving as additional eyes, ears, and sportsmanship role models) at local elementary and intermediate schools during recess.

K-1-2 helpers. Older elementary students have the capacity to help teachers of younger grades. Since elementary students don't have advisory periods like older kids, create a program where selected students come in before school to help teachers with organizational tasks (such as organizing folders or copies or helping update bulletin boards) or helping younger kids log into computers or practice spelling words or math facts.

Book buddies. There are a variety of ways to implement book buddy programs. For example, kids in third grade can be great partners to kindergartners, fourth graders with first graders, and so on, with kids from each grade (older and younger) taking turns reading and listening. You might even consider creating a mixed-grade book club for tweens and teens, with students working together to choose the books and lead the discussions. Regardless of how you partner grades, book buddy programs help strengthen fluency as well as build relationships.

Library aides. Starting in third or fourth grade, kids can serve as leaders in the library by helping peers choose and return books, reshelving books, and other library-related tasks. To ensure students meet the right skill level, create an application that asks them to sort books alphabetically and by the Dewey decimal system, and ask a few questions about why they want to be an aide. Conduct interviews so you are confident students will be able to confidently help peers who visit the library.

Buddy bench. This popular approach to addressing exclusion and loneliness on the playground involves having a designated bench or two where kids can sit if they're looking for someone to play with. Read the article "Wanted: Playground Buddy" at *Teaching Tolerance* to learn more (bit.ly/2HxtaAI). You can visit buddybench.org to get one started at your school. Students of any age can initiate this process.

Anti-bully buddies. If your school puts in place a buddy bench, you can organize a core group of kids who keep their eyes on the bench and are ready to join a student who sits on it. Ask the students to come up with a creative name for their group instead of "anti-bully buddies."

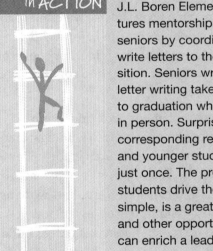

LEADERSHIP in ACTION

Letter Mentors

J.L. Boren Elementary School in Mansfield, Texas, nurtures mentorship between third graders and high school seniors by coordinating a pen pal program. Third graders write letters to the seniors to practice writing and composition. Seniors write back with questions and prompts. The letter writing takes place for the academic year until close to graduation when the pen pals finally meet each other in person. Surprisingly, the relationships students built by corresponding result in a strong bond between the older and younger students even though they interact in person just once. The process is facilitated by two teachers, but students drive the process. This type of program, though simple, is a great example of how mentoring, peer tutoring, and other opportunities where students help one another can enrich a leadership cultures.

The "School-Based Student Leadership Programs" table on page 100 shows at a glance the age of students who are best suited to conduct these student-led leadership programs and the age of recipients. Use the table to identify which programs might be appropriate for your setting.

LEADERSHIP *in ACTION*

Making Space to Speak

Student-driven leadership springs out of students recognizing their interdependence and interconnectedness with fellow students. And sometimes leadership lessons come not only from planning and carrying out events, but also from listening to the stories of others.

Another program in the Mansfield, Texas, school district is Mansfield Speaks, a TED talk–like event. This annual program arose when a group of students had an idea for students and staff in the high school to submit talk topics around specific themes such as "Perspective" and "Every Story Matters." A student board organizes the entire event, from soliciting proposals, conducting auditions, and selecting the student speakers to executing and MC-ing the well-attended event, which is held at a large performing arts center. Though every speech aligns with the overarching theme, parameters are loose enough to allow students to speak from the heart—and they've shared intimate stories about overcoming eating disorders, depression, growing up bilingual, losing loved ones, and their visions of the future.

The first year, the speeches included teachers and administrators. But after receiving feedback from the audience, the student board decided that the student speeches were more compelling, and now only students are eligible to try out. Knowing how busy students and families are, the event has been designed like an open house. Two weeks prior to the event, the list of selected speakers and their topics is announced, with an estimate of what time they'll be onstage. Some people stay for the entire event, others come to see specific students, and many people float between the lobby and the auditorium as the speakers they're interested in hearing step onstage. There have been student speakers who, until Mansfield Speaks came around, never tried out for anything, only to surprise the audience with stories so profound they're unforgettable.

Student government is another example of student-driven leadership, even if your school recognizes this organization as a club, because leaders and members are selected by their peers. It's most effective when advisors serve as leadership consultants and facilitators—guiding the student leadership team privately with the skills needed to lead their organization rather than instructing or teaching the entire membership.

If the results of your audit showed that very few student-driven leadership experiences exist, it's important to address the reasons: Why aren't students initiating programs to serve each other? Why are adults doing too much? Why don't we have new faces attending meetings? Why aren't more (girls, boys, students of color, athletes, underclassmen, and so on) getting involved, running for positions, or leading student organizations (or whatever gap your audit showed)?

Here are ideas for addressing these issues.

Encouraging Students to Serve Others

Often, the most successful leadership programs are created by students who identify a cause and are motivated to help. But if you don't have a robust student-driven leadership community, you can jump-start it. Survey older students to find out what leadership opportunities they are interested in, then follow through by identifying staff members who are willing to spearhead appropriate programs. Or show teachers the list of programs on pages 89–92 and ask for volunteers to launch one of their choosing. You might even consider requiring student participation in one of these programs if you have a leadership class or as part of earning a leadership letter (see page 111).

You can also do a "needs analysis" by asking teachers or administrators of kids in younger grades what they need. This ensures that you're allocating the time and energy to start programs that have a greater potential for success. Then start the program yourself—advertise for volunteers on the school website, on bulletin boards, in the morning announcements, and on hallway signs. Invite a core group of students to join and serve as enthusiastic initiators and ask teachers to talk up the opportunity with students.

Generally speaking, the most important strategy is to create an overwhelming and unmistakable leadership culture in your school. Make clear the value of community, the importance of volunteering and helping others, and the benefits of being a leader. If administrators and teachers are talking about leadership and community in and out of class, there's a good chance kids will feel motivated to do something.

Training Students to Serve Others

If your audit suggested there are problems with training for student-led leadership programs, it may be because adult leaders are indifferent or misaligned with the programs they're advising; they don't project a sense that the program is important; or, for some reason, they haven't made it a priority. Check in with these advisors and probe to find out what the issue is. If you can't get stronger buy-in from an advisor, you may need to replace him or her. You might even put a rotation in place, with teachers moving to advise different clubs or programs after a few years or semesters.

If students are approaching their roles unprepared, take a closer look at the training they're receiving. Preparing older students to serve younger students means training them for the content of the job they're doing—such as shelving library books or helping in class—and for responsible behavior around younger students. Remind them that they are role models for the younger kids. As most educators know, you may need to be explicit about what being a role model means to you—and to the students involved. Meet with adult advisors before they begin any training to discuss their approach and provide appropriate resources if advisors are inexperienced, are nervous, or could benefit from receiving leadership coaching of their own. Require adults to check in regularly with student leaders throughout their time in the program to troubleshoot any problems and reinforce their roles as resources for the student leaders they advise.

Attracting More Students to Student Government

If we want student government that truly represents the student body, we need many students to serve, including students from diverse populations. Work to increase the inclusiveness of student council at your school.

For example, if student government leaders at your school are chosen by administrators or teachers rather than students, you'll want to change. The same is true if only one student runs for president or other positions each year. Work with students to design a new format or approach to student government at your school. Recruit from leadership classes or create a pathway for students to start small to learn the ropes—on committees or as part of a group—moving into formal positions after getting some experience.

Some student councils select their current president and other positions halfway through the school year, with the new people becoming president-elect (vice president–elect, secretary-elect, and so on). The president-elect and other leaders-elect become apprentices to the current president throughout the second semester, taking over fully after spring break and into the next fall, with the cycle repeating itself every year. This can be a very effective approach because it gives emerging leaders time to ask questions and to learn their roles while providing partners to the current student leaders as they continue to lead the organization. This approach also creates greater sustainability and consistency and eliminates gaps in programming.

Encouraging All Kinds of Student Leaders

Being able to identify opportunities that appeal to every student hinges on understanding people of every age and from every walk of life.

In my experience, for good or bad, as educators we often think of students as belonging to one of three categories: doers, dreamers, and distractors. There are those who do—they make things happen. There are those who dream— they think about the big picture and possibility of making awesome things happen. And there are those who appear to distract—rough around the edges but with stamina and potential to serve as tipping points between the doers and dreamers.

Groups need kids with all three outlooks; no characteristic is better than the other! We often encourage the doers and dreamers but seek to keep distractors under control. But distractors aren't the same as "distracting." People in this category often remind teams to keep things fun. They use relationships to bring together tangential ideas and inspire balance between education and entertainment (a sort of work-life balance). They're natural entrepreneurs who possess an understanding (even if they don't realize it) that all work and no play make Jack and Janice dull leaders. Channeling the energy of distractors can lead to active engagement, the positive role of distractors. Clubs and teams thrive when they are made up of students in all three categories, and they *all* need the help of coaches and advisors who bring out their best.

Positions Are Still Important

While the overarching goal is to encourage students in general to get involved and develop common leadership behaviors, some individuals will want to go further. They'll seek identifiable, positional (that is, positions with *titles)* leadership roles that arise because they are nominated, selected, or voted in to a role that manages and leads others, makes authoritative decisions, holds responsibility for executing a project, and results in being recognized for their contributions. Therefore, it's important to maintain opportunities that require selection to positions that not everyone can hold. For people who are motivated by performance or following a process, earning or being selected to lead a group of peers or serve in a recognized leadership position can make a difference in their attitude and commitment to the group, club, or team.

LEADERSHIP in ACTION

A Community Service Day to Remember

High school students enrolled in one of my leadership classes spent months planning the school's first Community Service Day. The day was designed to dispatch every student into the community to volunteer at food banks, elementary schools, and nonprofits including Habitat for Humanity and community gardens. The idea was pitched by students, and I committed myself to facilitate rather than instruct, relinquishing power to the two young women selected as co-chairs.

Planning this event would have been a huge undertaking for a team of adults. It was considerably more challenging for the students because the school was an alternative school for students in the district considered at-risk for not graduating. Some students were teen parents, 40 percent were involved in gangs, 30 percent were identified as gifted (but with scant histories of receiving gifted services), another 30 percent had at one point received special education services, and 90 percent faced substance abuse issues—either their own or systemic in their families. "Serving others" was low on their list of priorities. Students who had previously participated in community service had done so to earn hours to get off probation.

The co-chairs organized and managed committees charged with finding nonprofits and community groups for 250+ volunteer spots. They worked with me to design a comprehensive preservice, in-service, and reflection process; they distributed the required permission slips, waivers, and risk-management documents; and they trained peers to serve as team leaders when on site. They also contacted multiple news outlets to cover the event. Their PR pitch focused on how teens who many perceived as troublesome were doing good and being leaders in their community.

The day was an incredible success. The Habitat for Humanity site contacted the co-chairs midway through to say how the team of twenty-five boys (that's right, twenty-five teen boys, most of whom were active gang members) was the best team they'd had in a long time. But as the day wrapped up and service teams congregated at the school to debrief and celebrate, the co-chairs grew frustrated that none of the news channels or reporters had showed up at the sites or at the closing activity (a student band was tapped for entertainment). We soon found out why: Less than twenty-five miles away, the Columbine shooting was unfolding. Reporters who weren't at their stations were headed there.

The co-chairs quickly switched from lamenting the lack of news promotion to understanding that there were students at another high school who were running for their lives. I asked them if they wanted to end differently than they'd planned—with prizes and a student band playing—because celebrating might feel insensitive. The leaders weighed pros and cons of celebrating the unprecedented contributions they'd made that day or telling their class-mates about Columbine (this was before social media, and the general student population had no idea what was happening).

Within minutes, they made a measured, mature decision. They felt so much ownership of the event that they continued with the celebration. They wanted the enthusiasm and deep connections made among teams from spending a day actively and positively contributing to their home community to be what everyone remembered. As they said, "In a bit, everyone'll go home and hear about the horrible event that happened there, while we were making a difference here. No one will talk about today except all of us. We're not ready to go back to feeling less than, like today never happened. So let's celebrate and have the band play. After school is out, everyone can go back out into the real world." I hugged them both and said, "You're supported 100 percent."

They extended the magic of their event so this gathering—*their* gathering—of normally disengaged teens could revel in a day of transforming their community and themselves. They weren't ignoring what was happening beyond their school, but they knew there was nothing they could do to change it. They prioritized their stakeholders, they recognized the contributions of everyone involved in the event, and they made thoughtful decisions despite an unprecedented situation taking place elsewhere. They made difficult choices, evaluated possibilities, and acted with integrity—just what we hope for when students are prepared and supported to lead their organizations.

SCHOOL-BASED STUDENT LEADERSHIP PROGRAMS

	K	1st	2nd	3rd	4th	5th	6th	7th	8th	9th	10th	11th	12th
Student athlete outreach													
Student assistants/teacher aides													
Teacher cadets/student teachers													
Middle/high school transition teams, ninth-grade ambassadors													
Girls/boys leadership mentors, mixed-gender social-skills/friendship mentoring groups													
Principal's advisory council													
Peer tutors													
Peer helpers/mediators													
Honor society team helpers													
Activity monitors/playground partners													
K-1-12 helpers													
Book buddies													
Library aides (high schoolers may be teacher assistants)													
Buddy bench													
Anti-bullying buddies													

KEY

— Indicates target students as resources (students serving as mentors, tutors, role models, etc.)

Shaded areas indicate target student recipients

······I Emphasis is on older elementary students helping younger

From *Leadership Is a Life Skill* by Mariam G. MacGregor, M.S., copyright © 2018. This page may be reproduced for individual, classroom, or small group work only. For all other uses, contact Free Spirit Publishing Inc. at www.freespirit.com/permissions.

CHAPTER 7
Student Support Programs and General Social-Emotional Learning (SEL)

Social-emotional learning (SEL) and character education efforts can be invaluable parts of your leadership culture in your school or district. Leadership, at its core, is about understanding social and emotional cues, using SEL skills, and showing positive character. The more kids learn about SEL and character, the better prepared they are to be leaders.

If you have an SEL or character education program already in place at your school, you don't need to make big changes, but you do want to make sure you're maximizing the leadership lessons. This chapter provides strategies for doing so. If you don't have any programs like these, I recommend starting one; use the ideas in this chapter to determine where to start and what to prioritize as you build it.

In addition to SEL and character education, leadership training can be an effective way to directly and indirectly address bullying at your school. Finally, you may choose to launch a class devoted specifically to leadership to use classroom time to focus more directly and intensely on this subject. This clearly emphasizes dedication to creating a leadership culture at your school, since you are literally making it part of the curriculum. You'll find tips for setting up the class and some suggested resources for curriculum starting on page 110.

Building Great SEL, Character Education, and Other Support Programs

SEL and character education programs—and other programs such as anti-bullying and drug and alcohol programs—may overlap with one another in terms of content, and all these may overlap with a leadership class. For example, meaningfully designed leadership classes often include character education elements, teach self-advocacy skills, and explore how to challenge bullying. This means students in the leadership class can be trained to serve as small-group leaders if you conduct a separate school-wide bullying prevention program, instead of sitting in the audience. It's okay to allow for some overlap, but be cautious about overwhelming students, parents, and teachers, ultimately diluting the messages of all the programs.

While teaching SEL (and similar topics) inherently promotes leadership lessons, you can do more to enhance the leadership message and encourage leadership behaviors. Topics like empathy, compassion, and citizenship provide obvious openings for students to take the lead in helping others. If your audit showed that student support programs need improvement or are an opportunity for building leadership lessons, here are some strategies for beefing them up.

Meet the Needs of All Students

Ideally your audit shed light on some of the awesome work already being done at your school or in your district. It also might have revealed that some kids are exposed to multiple social-emotional growth opportunities and others are not. While no one intends to leave out any students, it happens. If this is true in your setting, look for ways to strategically expand your program or add a new one.

Students on the path of being first-generation graduates in their families may find it hard to get involved in co-curricular leadership activities. Some students may have responsibilities at home or a job. One way to reach these students is by offering SEL opportunities during regularly scheduled academic classes or leadership classes. Encourage these students to enroll in classes that will address SEL and leadership—these opportunities likely align with their ambition and fit into the normal school day.

For example, a student in a leadership class I taught didn't fully invest until she was promoted to assistant manager at a local Dairy Queen. She was only 17, yet the manager was asking her to hire and fire people older than her. After the promotion, she used class activities and journaling to help find ways to handle employees. If learning leadership skills had only been available through clubs, her thirty-hour work week (plus full-time school) would have prevented her from gaining the leadership skills that helped her succeed.

When a sense of survival is at stake, helping kids connect leadership to resilience (an essential social-emotional skill) can change lives. Students living in poverty or in abusive households may feel a sense of disconnect when being urged or taught to self-advocate. They might seem resistant to leading or believe they aren't leaders. It's important to make the concept of leadership feel real to them. For kids like this, it's important to present learning to lead as a life skill necessary to handle difficult situations.

Provide Opportunities to Use What They Learn

One of the best ways to build leadership skills is to *use* them. Consider these ways to actively engage your students who are in SEL and other support programs.

Peer programs. Encourage students to start or volunteer for peer leadership programs such as those discussed in chapter 6 (pages 89–92). For example, older students might:

- build, install, or decorate friendship benches on your playground, where kids who want to provide extra support take turns helping other kids who need a dose of support or someone to play with

- act as ambassadors who greet new students or guests visiting the school

- lead orientation and support and mentor other students as they move up in grades

- volunteer as activity and game leaders or refs (like camp counselors) during recess for younger students, or help at annual events like field days

Filling buckets. For younger students studying SEL, have teachers read the book *Have You Filled a Bucket Today?* by Carol McCloud to the class and discuss with students how leaders help fill buckets. Place large plastic buckets around the school or in individual classrooms, or ask your art teacher to have students decorate pint-size buckets for their desks. Provide scratch paper and markers for kids and teachers to write positive affirmation notes (or "bucket fillers") to others. Review the notes and read them once a week during school announcements. One way to introduce this concept is to use it as a theme for a school-wide Leadership Day. (You can find information on Leadership Day on pages 136–143 and the "Have You Filled a Bucket Today?" theme on page 140.)

Principal's advisory board. Starting around third grade, students value being included in decision-making activities that directly affect their school experience. To affirm students as leadership resources and partners, invite student representatives from your SEL classes from all grades and different interest areas to be part of a principal's (or superintendent's, depending on your role) advisory board. See page 40 for more information.

Student-led workshops. Have students plan and conduct at least one workshop on a social-emotional learning topic (such as building empathy or empathetic leadership, conflict resolution, inclusion, dealing with frustration, or dealing with test anxiety) for any school- or district-wide professional development days each year.

Creative space. Have students develop a designated "creative space"—for example, a reconfigurable room with moveable furniture, sliding white boards, and technology hookups—on campus that can serve as an incubator lab or idea factory. In this space, students may come together from different grades in the same school or even from across the district to brainstorm ways to improve the school or district. They can loop in district decision makers too. In some schools, the theater or practice gym can serve as this flex space. Social-emotional learning occurs through students' effectively managing the room and its use, and imposing consequences if others disrespect the space.

LEADERSHIP in ACTION

Vending Changes

Students in one school district were dissatisfied with the junk food stocked in their vending machines, so they spent one day a week for six weeks in their district's "innovation space," meeting with district nutrition experts, the district contracts manager (the contract with the vending machine provider was nearing its end), and the superintendent's office to design an RFP (request for proposal) for a new vendor. The students used the same space for presentations before selecting the winning vendor. Students established community rules for how to reserve the room and guidelines for using the room, for example, the expected condition of the room after use—trash cleaned up, chairs organized, tables cleaned.

Combine Leadership and SEL Opportunities Outside of Program Time

There are a variety of ways to organically and informally infuse leadership development into students' lives. Here are some ways to do it:

- Use occasional advisory periods to conduct leadership activities and mini-lessons focused on building a pro-social community and not tied to a specific academic subject. You can also pair up students to develop leadership lessons, icebreakers, or team-builders to facilitate, putting them in charge of leading the session and discussion.

- Provide regular counselor time for younger students. Have counselors meet with small groups or classrooms of kids to introduce leadership and soft-skills concepts. Counselors at some elementary schools create "friendship groups" to put together kids who struggle socially with kids who confidently navigate friendships. These groups meet once or twice a month and take the form of private activities (like group therapy settings), eating together at lunch, volunteering for an at-school service activity, or working together on a project during the friendship group time.

- Facilitate leadership initiatives and problem-solving activities such as Trust Walk, Spider Web, TP Shuffle (or any number of ones you'll find when searching the internet for "low-challenge course activities," "team-building activities," or leadership games") during recess to build teamwork and communication skills. If any of your playgrounds are scheduled to be renovated, consider redesigning traditional monkey-bar and swing spaces to include low-challenge course elements as permanent structures where students can create their own leadership-skill-building games too. But every recess shouldn't revolve around an organized leadership game, because unstructured time allows students to organically apply leadership skills by negotiating and resolving conflicts without adults.

- Change mindsets and attitudes by conducting leadership development during detention or other time slots previously reserved for punishment. Instead of having students do nothing but get angry as an outcome of negative behavior or poor social skills, engage and prepare students who might otherwise be overlooked or excluded from existing leadership programs or classes.

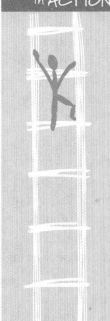

LEADERSHIP in **ACTION**

E.P.I.C. (Every Person Is a Champion) Peer Mentors

The previously mentioned Red Rocks Elementary builds leadership culture in student support programs in a noteworthy way. It started with a fourth-grade student who volunteered with Night Lights, a community nonprofit organization serving families of kids with special needs. As a third grader, he'd been the reading buddy of a younger student enrolled in the district-wide special needs program housed at the school. Whenever the younger student with special needs had a hard day, teachers discovered that his reading buddy helped calm him down. Other students started asking if they could help too.

The student decided to start an academic and social mentoring program to serve other kids in the special needs program. He approached Mr. Austin, a universally favorite teacher, to help. Mr. Austin embraced the idea and worked with the student to organize selection, training, administrative support, and public relations with teachers and parents (of students with special needs and of the students interested in being mentors). Having a student start the program was notable. So were the mutually meaningful relationships made between the kids with special needs and their mentors.

One unexpected impact of the program came when self-submitting applications were announced and a sixth-grade student who had never tried out for, run for, or been involved in anything at the school applied. When more students applied than could be selected, Red Rocks stayed committed to finding ways students could serve as peer helpers to students needing academic or social support in any grade.

Meet Mr. Austin and learn more at bit.ly/2FAcImM.

Using Leadership to Address Bullying Behaviors

A tremendous amount of time and energy is dedicated to bullying prevention. Sometimes, this emphasis on bully-proofing kids overshadows preparing them to appropriately confront peers, resolve conflicts, self-advocate, and be resourceful in social situations. For some kids, parents have quickly stepped in to complain to teachers or work managers or coaches on their kids' behalves, eliminating opportunities for kids to learn these skills. But all kids can learn to deal with bullying through an understanding of leadership skills and by being a leader.

Encourage Conflict Resolution and Standing Up

When leadership culture and behavior expectations become school-wide, it sets the tone that every student can be competent at problem-solving. In a school with such a tone, students strive to resolve conflict situations in socially healthy and appropriate ways without strong adult intervention. Implement a way to recognize students who stand up and speak out about bullying—they are using leadership skills and appealing to your school's shared leadership values. This might include "Awesome" awards that kids can fill in and present to peers, weekly "Peer Hero" or "Random Act of Kindness" awards presented by and to teachers or students, and earning tokens or tickets to put in a drawing for prizes once a month or semester (depending on the age of kids).

A program like Ben's Bells Step Up! (see page 66) can be effective because it trains and supports kids to choose positive behaviors and to stand up to help others who might be experiencing bullying.

Process for Reporting

Unfortunately, sometimes peer-to-peer leadership interventions don't work and situations can rise to the level where adults need to get involved. Knowing this, design and implement a process for students to work with adults or your leadership advisory team to safely report bullying and get a response. Some schools set up anonymous tip lines to call or text, others use confidential surveys to collect information and identify locations in or near the school where bullying occurs. (Check out Qualtrics K–12 Innovation Community for resources on data collection: www.qualtrics.com/education/innovation-k12.) No matter what reporting method you put in place, it's imperative to include the information on school websites and any social media accounts students and parents may access.

Bullying Response Team

Some schools select high school students and train them with crisis leadership skills to serve as a "bully response team." The team visits elementary and middle schools to work with small groups of students. If you lead an elementary school, consider implementing friendship groups (see page 105) to give kids who might be targets their own team of upstander peers. Pacer's National Bullying Prevention Center has extensive resources for the classroom and for setting up student intervention teams (www.pacer.org/bullying).

Books and Movies

You can use books or movies that present leadership as a foil to bullying.

- **For younger kids, read aloud or have students read the book *Just Kidding* by Trudy Ludwig.** This book focuses on how kids justify demeaning or belittling comments by saying that their mean comment was just a joke.

- **You can use the same book as a resource with older kids too.** Teens often text or say things like, "Relax, dude—JK" to friends. The book can help teen leaders grasp how sarcasm and mocking others can be seen as passive-aggressive by others. Exploring this behavior also builds more complex social-emotional self-awareness and expectations of accountability for older teens. As teens mature, it's important to help them understand how easily bullying can become manipulation and the role good leaders can play in preventing this from happening.

- **For teens, movie choices are abundant.** Ranging from classics like *The Goonies* (rated PG) and *The Breakfast Club* (rated R mainly for profanity) and semi-classics like *Mean Girls* (rated PG-13), to more recent titles such as *Wonder* (rated PG) and *The Greatest Showman* (rated PG), movies offer engaging ways to learn leadership techniques to handle bullying and navigate the social pecking order.

Champions for Those with Special Needs

Many schools offer "Partners in PE" or "Partners in Art" peer mentoring for kids with special needs such as sensory processing disorder or autism spectrum disorder who attend traditional schools. Programs like these train typically developing students to support and be champions for their peers with special needs, particularly students whose special needs may not be immediately obvious to other peers. Because of their leadership role, students trained as partners can reinforce your culture of leadership by modeling how to act with greater patience and understanding. So instead of a child being picked on because he or she lacks appropriate social skills, runs slower in PE, or has unexplainable quirks or behaviors, the child's partner rallies around him or her and sets a classroom standard where bullying is deemed unacceptable.

Shift in Attitude

When you emphasize leadership as a tool to address bullying, a natural shift in student and adult attitudes toward misbehavior occurs. Students begin paying attention to peers who are leading and making good decisions instead of seeing only the ways others "wrongly" treat them. Kids learn to manage bullying as part of a larger group—as a "strength in numbers" social collective—rather than with secrecy or individual suffering.

Building a Leadership Class

A dedicated leadership class is a great way to put focus on leadership concepts and go beyond traditional event planning and spirit. These classes are easiest to offer in middle and high school when most schools begin to offer elective options. One semester provides enough time to thoroughly teach leadership concepts and build a strong team atmosphere. After the semester, students will be ready to launch into leadership roles, advanced leadership classes like Community Leadership (see a sample syllabus: bit.ly/2IXbQGR), or project-driven leadership classes where students address a concern or challenge in their school or community. An example of the latter is on page 105, "Leadership in Action: Vending Changes."

In elementary school, leadership classes can be a club option, especially if your school offers ongoing weekly clubs. Teach one leadership lesson each time the club meets until the full curriculum is complete.

When evaluating who's the best teacher for your leadership class, find an enthusiastic person interested in making leadership and its real-life applications come alive for students. Teacher-coaches often value teaching this topic because it closely aligns with the atmosphere they're building on teams. So do history teachers, English teachers, school counselors, AVID teachers, art teachers, career-tech teachers, and . . . well, there's not *one* right teacher.

Reach a Wide Audience

Strive to fill the class with diverse voices and experiences, not just the kids who typically love to join causes. To avoid having only the usual suspects sign up, extend direct invitations from counselors, advisors, coaches, and school leaders to enroll students who reflect a variety of perspectives.

Build a Rigorous Curriculum

Like you would with any syllabus, seek to align lessons with a set of standards on leadership. These can be tied to a rubric you design focused on strengthening competence in the skills identified in chapter 1 (pages 19–22) or standards specific to leadership classes (like these developed by the National Association of Student Councils: bit.ly/2pf0QLQ).

You might even consider teaching an interdisciplinary leadership class, where teachers from different subject areas rotate into the class each week to teach leadership concepts tied to their subject area expertise. If you want to teach a leadership class focused on service and social change, see page 110 for a Community Leadership syllabus.

Take It a Step Further

When building leadership cultures, it's important to identify unique ways to recognize or showcase the leadership development of students. Because leadership skills are a demonstration of social-emotional learning in action, you're striving to recognize a collection of behaviors, not just a "hero" who responded a single time as a leader or excelled at doing just one thing. Here are two ways to achieve this:

Letter in leadership. Like a letter in athletics or fine arts, offer a leadership letter that is based on achieving certain benchmarks such as taking certain leadership classes, the number of volunteer hours worked, involvement in mentoring or peer tutoring activities, academic achievement, random acts of kindness, serving as an orientation leader or other roles in your school or district, participation in clubs and co-curricular activities (including fine arts and athletics), representing the definition of leadership as developed by your school or district, and making a legacy impact. You can align your program with the standards, both similar and unique, for earning your school's athletic letter. Or you can model it after the approach created by leadership developers DECA: www.decadirect.org/2013/10/15/the -deca-letter-motivate-and-recognize-excellence-in-leadership.

Leadership portfolio. Students can compile a portfolio (online or in another format) that archives their leadership activities throughout their school experiences. Their leadership portfolios can include photos, videos, project plans, or journal entries related to extracurricular activities, mentoring, community service, events they planned, committees on which they served, and so forth. Google Drive is one place to have students begin their archiving, because many students set up their initial account in second or third grade, and Google has an e-portfolio tool. WordPress is another platform to consider, because blogging strengthens writing skills, and you can activate the portfolio plug-in to track leadership learning.

Because technology changes rapidly, research e-portfolio platforms to find one that's best for your goals. For college-bound students, a detailed leadership portfolio can serve as a terrific reference point when filling out college applications. For students entering the military or workforce directly after graduation, having a leadership portfolio can set them apart by demonstrating an ongoing commitment to leadership.

THREE

PART 3
TAKING THE LONG VIEW

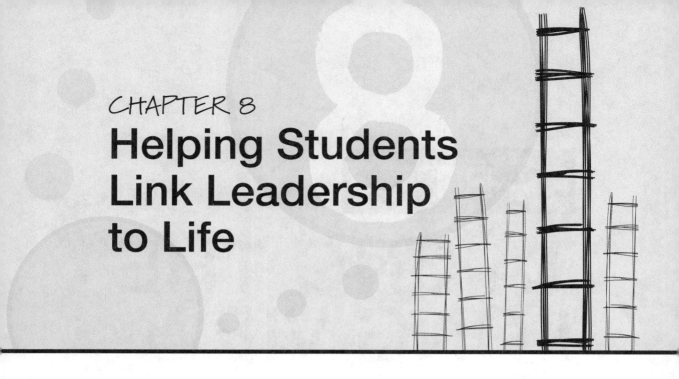

CHAPTER 8
Helping Students Link Leadership to Life

Ask kindergartners what they want to be when they grow up and you'll get straightforward and simple responses: a fire fighter, doctor, lawyer, teacher, professional athlete—or whatever job their mother or father does. Ask middle school students what they want to be when they grow up, and the response time is slower. They might say "I'm not sure" or name a job connected to subject areas they really like—art or writing or math or science. Maybe they've identified fields they might want to enter, such as technology, medicine, acting, or professional athletics (that one rarely falls off the list). By the time students are preparing for high school graduation, their responses are more illuminated, even if accompanied by doubt: "I want to be a mechanic," "I plan to attend law school," "I'm exploring careers where I can be outside or be active."

Responses and post-secondary paths will vary. But for students who experienced leadership cultures in school, paths will share a commonality. They'll not only have the adaptability to learn new technical skills and knowledge on the job, but their leadership skills and self-awareness will set them apart as someone others like to work with. As the use of technology increases, having irreplaceable "human-only" skills at a job can make or break success. In other words, skills that technology can't replace—everything we've covered in this book—make people better classmates and colleagues. Possessing these skills can also make a person more likely to be hired and promoted.

As students near graduation, it's important to help them make the connection between their leadership skills and college/career success. Here are some techniques to promote with your staff that will help this connection gel organically for students.

Be Socially Intelligent

A natural assumption, right? But often adults overlook the fact that our attitudes as educators must reflect the same socially intelligent competencies we seek in students. Maintaining a positive attitude, apologizing when we're at fault, inviting kids into conversations with adults or mixed audiences, helping students learn to "read a room," and establishing expectations for accountability and responsibility are elemental actions modeled by socially intelligent adults.

Seek to Understand Kids' Social Politics at School

Even parents and teachers who easily build rapport with kids find that some students are less forthcoming than others when asked about social dynamics and peer interactions. In fact, nearly every kid goes through a period of keeping their social life private—good, bad, and otherwise—from adults. That's why adults need to craft questions that evoke more than yes/no responses.

It's also helpful to visit the cafeteria or playgrounds at your school somewhat regularly to chat and play with students (if you're a district administrator, encourage the principals at their schools to do so). When visiting, be conscientious about not standing around with all the adults as if doing surveillance! When you observe small groups congregating, notice what they're doing and how they're treating others around them. Engage with groups without being intrusive or dorky—modeling social intelligence leads to gaining trust and learning more about the daily social politics taking place informally.

In primary classrooms, doing a daily temperature check in the morning, midday, and later in the afternoon can reveal how well kids are getting along in the classroom. Teachers can ask things like:

- How is the table you sit at in class working?
- Who do you like sitting with at lunch?

- Who do you wish you got to talk to or play with today? (And then set aside time each day to allow quick connections that fulfill this desire.)
- Were people getting along during recess?
- What can happen tomorrow to make your school day better than it was today?

With teens, the conversations will take place quickly and possibly in passing. You might ask:

- How were the halls today between classes?
- How was so-and-so's class?
- Any challenges going on with your group project?
- What do you think of the [fill in the blank] thread on [Twitter, Facebook, Snapchat, other social media platform]?

Understanding social politics is not about finding ways to lecture or giving advice; it's about listening quietly and without judgment to what kids and teens are saying and finding ways to subtly promote social-emotional awareness and leadership skills as helpful navigation tools.

Recognize the Impact of Social Politics Outside School

Social politics keep going after the school bell. When students head to sports practice, clubs, and hanging out with friends, the social navigating they do is like what they do during the school day. Sometimes after school is more challenging, because students are dealing with private networking and the possibility of being part of the "in crowd" or being excluded through text and group chats. Coaches and advisors can ask questions (and listen carefully to the responses) about who's doing what, how friends are spending their time together, what's new in the lives of others, how things went during and after practice, where students perceive themselves to fit in the hierarchy, who leads trends and attitudes, and more. We can check in on rumors and gossip being heard from students to encourage open communication, increase leadership influence, and prevent subversive peer pressure.

PART 3

Stay Focused and Engaged

Remember new names when they become part of the conversation. Listen fully when students describe who's hanging out together and where it puts them in the social pecking order. If necessary, prompt them to describe their feelings about it. Watch their faces and body language so you can read nonverbal cues. This models empathetic leadership and encourages similar behavior from kids and teens when they interact with one another.

Reinforce Practice

Like everything else we want to get better at doing, we must practice leadership behaviors and put soft skills through a regular workout. For example, practice ways with your class to confront inappropriate social behaviors among friends. Let students know that individually they don't always have to be the "grown-up in the room," but that when necessary, you support them to speak up against peers that go too far with power or group think. (Or, as I say to students and my own kids, know when to fully engage your frontal lobe!) Practice creative thinking by asking students to teach various topics to the class. They can choose from lessons on pages 144–148 or other leadership lessons you find. You can also provide students with the leadership characteristics handout (pages 19–22) and partner with them to find new ways to tie these concepts to existing lessons.

Allow Transition Time

Whether students are transitioning from one classroom to the next or just between activities or subjects in class, most students value having three to five minutes (beyond hallway passing periods) to interact with peers, chatter and make noise, be in motion, and generally wind down from the mental and emotional high and low of the previous task. Squeeze a few minutes into the break between subjects (if students stay in the same room) or at the start of your class (if students are coming from different classes, as most middle and high school students do).

Transition time allows brief moments of decompression throughout the day. If topics discussed in their previous classes or activities remain at the forefront of their minds, transition time allows for a shift similar to "clicking" to a new webpage. For younger students who may not switch classrooms, allow time for a quick brain break by using GoNoodle or some other silly and fun activity that gets them laughing and emotionally connecting with one another. And because relationships and connections with others influence social intelligence, transition time enhances students' abilities to remember that the world (and classroom) doesn't revolve only around them.

Respect Disappointment and Failure

Succeeding after failure requires more than picking oneself up to try again. It's also tied to attitude and outlook. People generally fall into two loose categories, or depending on situations or circumstances, swing between the two: "the world is out to get me," an attitude of pessimism and protection, or "the world is out there!" an attitude of optimism and opportunity. The more we push kids toward the latter, the more resilient and self-assured they will be after an attempt at something (a relationship, an audition, an interview, and so on) goes wrong.

Many college students and first-time job applicants are inept at dealing with failure because they haven't been allowed to fail. Or they define failure as getting a B in a class where they expected—they usually say *deserved*—an A. Significant social-emotional growth is achieved when students learn to manage disappointment through their *own* resourcefulness and recovery. Instead of saving them, educators and influential adults in leadership cultures *must* let students fail forward. Learning from mistakes can be difficult, but the lessons can stick for life.

Coach for Constructive Confidence

The world is full of smart adults, with millions of smart kids rising through the ranks ready to take their place. But there's a difference between a confident intellectual who possesses soft skills and a person who's brilliant and wants everyone to know it. People who are soft-skill savvy would rather be wrong about something than ruin a friendship. A smart person who lacks social intelligence shouldn't get a "pass" by adults who overlook egotistical behavior because of someone's intelligence. What that person needs most is honest feedback, such as, "You can be right all the time, or you can have friends; you can't do both" or "Strive hard to do your best the first time, unless you have time to do it over."

This coaching is as much for the student as it is for current and future peers, colleagues, and bosses who interact with the student. Differentiate between constructive confidence and destructive arrogance.

Leadership cultures embedded in the K–12 experience can protect society from perpetuating boorish, jerk-like behavior from coworkers and leaders by giving feedback and teaching communication skills early on. Nurture thoughtful, coachable individuals in the world, and help young leaders become skilled enough to do the same.

Encourage Retelling and Revising of Life Stories

Everyone develops a story over the course of their lives. When kids experience high-stress households or difficult circumstances, their stories may begin to feel burdensome or impossible to overcome. Even individuals who have fought through setbacks in life but achieved success find comfort in falling back to their old stories.

It's helpful to remember that even the best novels (movies, TV shows, and so on) go through multiple revisions and stages of editorial review. Likewise, while educators can't change their students' experiences or the actual events they've been through, they can encourage students to "write their future stories," giving voice to past experiences while they imagine what their life *can* become. This process often provides relief to kids or teens who seek to let go of difficult aspects of their childhoods by introducing a new, self-directed perspective.

Other kids who may struggle with their internal narrator are those who excel in academics, sports, or another talent but who long to pursue interests outside the confines of how others view them. As individuals mature, some want to take control of future chapters of their stories to overcome circumstances that are holding them back.

Make time for personal reflection and opportunities to recalculate one's trajectory. Create daily writing prompts about life—have students write about something that makes them unique, a situation that they wish had gone differently, a disappointment they've faced, or what they wish others knew about them. If you use daily prompts, consider posting the entire month's list of prompts at the front of the room so students have time for extended reflection, especially if you ask questions that evoke greater vulnerability. You could also organize activities in your classroom around monthlong themes like "What's my story?" or "Every story matters."

Challenge the Status Quo

As much as people complain about the status quo, they generally accept it. New ideas are pitched and everyone resists. If "we always do it like this" or "that will never work" sound familiar, or if you feel that nothing in your district ever changes, then there's work to do. Learning to challenge the status quo is how students can learn to succeed in the workplace as well.

- As a way of modeling inclusion, choose the kid no one else would consider to lead an activity.

- Invite the student who others are unsure of or who may have struggled socially earlier in their K–12 experience to start a new club.

- Encourage kids and teens to assume positive intent when new ideas are pitched by team members or other students in class or on projects, and do the same with colleagues.

- Don't be afraid to challenge existing traditions and start new ones.

Follow Social Media

I'm not suggesting friending students or tweeting personal opinions and social complaints! Following social media and keeping up with the newest memes, apps, and online games isn't to make you cool—it's to make you aware. Nurturing social-emotional growth relies on skillfully speaking the same social language as students. Instagram, Snapchat, Twitter, YouTube, and other social networks are reliable sources of entertaining content for kids and teens; they can also be the source of overly simplified "news" and social commentary. By paying attention to the online lives of teens, you can ask questions when students repeat incomplete snippets or sound bites of a story. This sets the stage for deeper conversation and opportunities to learn more about topics, especially if what students repeat is inaccurate. Teachers and college professors are concerned that kids who grow up getting news and information primarily from social media may have a hard time discerning fact from fiction. Being knowledgeable of where kids and teens are getting information and talking openly or teaching critical thinking skills can shift this tide.

Be Available Through Multiple Forms of Communication

Connecting student leadership development to college and career success requires modeling good communication skills. Setting only in-person office hours may be convenient to you as the adult leader, but emerging generations value micro-feedback and connection through text and apps. Kids are online and on devices. (However, many kids don't regularly check email. To compensate for this, colleges increasingly use texts, apps, and personalized portals to communicate with students.) Many students like receiving assignments and test reminders by push notifications (such as Remind). Schools or individual teachers that rely on traditional paper communication or use minimal technology with students create unnecessary barriers to success.

Honor Each New School Year

We all naturally prefer it when what we did in the past works year after year. However, every group of students is different. Be ready and willing to adapt— to teach material differently, talk about topics you may not have discussed before, and start the year without assumptions about how students will interact or lead.

Prepare Students for Firsts

First day at a new school. First day at a camp where they know no one. First date. First formal concert. First losing game that counts. First winning game that counts. First day after graduation or at college. First interview. First internship. First day at their first job. First day at their second job. Each of these firsts carries with it different expectations for behavior. Some firsts happen easily and organically, like making friends at camp or at school. Some firsts, like interviewing for a job (and working at that job), require coaching and preparation from adults who care.

This coaching and preparation for life's firsts will be inherent in the leadership culture you create at school and can be explicitly taught in classrooms, in school clubs and organizations, on sports teams, and at jobs. Start early with a friendship group for young students in which they learn how to shake hands, introduce themselves, and engage in empathetic conversation (listening to learn, not listening to respond).

Strive for the Common Good

Starting when students are young—and being consistent throughout their K–12 experience—coach students to feel empathy and to care for something greater than themselves. Give them opportunities to feel the value of being a contributor or on a team. Nobody likes working with someone who appears self-centered; it can be hard to trust such a person. But team players and leaders who appreciate the greater good are likely to be supported and championed and experience greater long-term success. That message is central to everything this book is about, and I consider it one of the most important investments we can make as influencers in the K–12 experience.

CHAPTER 9
Tips to Be a Transformative Leader

Over the twenty-plus years I've been engaged in leadership education, I have kept a small notebook for jotting down observations and ideas—what works, what doesn't, and how to maintain direction while spearheading leadership revolutions within large populations of educators and students. If you're reading this book, most likely you are a significant—if not the most significant—influencer in your setting for creating such a revolution. Consider this chapter a "greatest hits" from my notebooks: final thoughts to inspire you throughout the transformation.

Establish a Personal Board of Advisors (BoA)

When I embark on making significant changes in any setting, I find building a like-minded support system to be invaluable. My support system consists of a diverse group of mentors and colleagues, including students, who understand what's going to be involved in achieving the change. I don't hold formal meetings or assign titles, and many of the people never meet each other in person, but I consider them my "personal board of advisors." The people I rely on may change over time and by situation, but there are several folks (including former students) who've been on my BoA for more than twenty years! When creating a board of advisors, select people who will both challenge your ideas *and* empower or encourage you, because they care personally about you and your success.

Be on a Quest for Curiosity, Creativity, and Critical Thinking

It sounds obvious that one would prioritize these three desirable workplace competencies, yet the pressure of (and policy makers' devotion to) collecting data and driving learning based on that data has narrowed the flexibility of teachers to use all three to teach all three! This book presents a variety of ideas to emphasize curiosity *and* accountability. The quest can be personally challenging—for example, when students with mentoring and leadership roles make unexpected mistakes, can you put aside any frustration to skillfully guide them? Recognize the creativity, curiosity, or critical thinking that most likely influenced the mistake. Remind yourself how hard it is to learn something new. Feel and express deep empathy, remembering what you were like at that student's age and responding in a way that reflects what *you* most needed to hear from a teacher or mentor at that time.

For all of us, the road to becoming a leader will be paved with mistakes. Growing from those mistakes requires adaptability and a foundation of creative and critical thinking.

Encourage Out-of-the-Box Thinking

This buzz phrase has been around a long time because it works. When people feel free to try new things—without fear of reprisal, that is—the results can be incredible. If you as the leader find yourself saying, "That won't work" or "We tried that, and it failed," challenge your assumptions. And then call someone on your personal BoA to help rebalance your outlook.

Embrace Spontaneity

Life occurs daily (duh), which means opportunities for leadership lessons happen daily too. Rigid insistence that we stick to a lesson plan overlooks opportunities to explore leadership-relevant issues that might crop up, such as national or global current events; points raised in a book being read in class;

or unique or pivotal events happening close to home, such as the death of a student or teacher, town elections, or a local controversy.

Kids of all ages value discussions that are real, relevant, and revealing. Make issues relevant to students by asking questions like, "What would you do if that happened to you?" or "What do you think this leader could do?" or "How does this align with how we've defined leadership?"

Be "Flashy"

A favorite element of leadership development sessions I do with administrators is teaching them how to facilitate "flash" lessons. These short, engaging activities, which get students moving and focused on a leadership concept, are made even more powerful by you—the administrator (principal, superintendent, etc.)—visiting the class to surprise students by teaching them. You probably have some great ideas of your own, and if not, you can find plenty of examples online and in leadership curriculum books. I like this formula for flash lessons: Start with a few minutes of student interaction with each other followed by a few discussion questions. Then close with a connection to a leadership topic or theme specific to the group, your school, or a top-of-mind idea associated with the class subject matter. In all cases, the most effective sessions come from principals or upper-level leaders willing to be "real" by respectfully incorporating your personality—self-deprecating, humble, entertaining, or funny.

Work out your visit with the classroom teacher ahead of time, of course (but ask them to act surprised when you arrive!).

Show Up and Engage

When I attend school events and various awards ceremonies, I observe how frontline leaders (principals, coaches, favorite teachers, superintendents) interact with students. It's a compelling way to figure out how authentically leaders connect with the broad student population throughout the school year. More than once it's been evident that a principal isn't genuinely connected to his or her students, which leads to incredibly awkward small talk with parents or students. Principals who stay cloistered in their office—who don't walk the halls, visit classes, do playground or bus duty—miss out on modeling the leadership culture they want to achieve. Students and teachers respond positively to the ones who do. They can count on seeing their principal regularly—in the halls, at events, cheering at competitions. Students and staff with engaged principals or other administrators experience a strong sense of connection and genuine belief that their administrator cares for them. Engaged administrators feel the pulse of what's happening in their schools. They're better informed and prepared to handle unpredictable situations. Engaged administrators also have an easier time providing professional feedback to teachers, implementing big decisions that directly affect the campus culture, and communicating potentially controversial changes because they've visibly and emotionally walked alongside their students and staff all along.

Tap *Your* Backyard Experts

School districts and communities are filled with underappreciated experts. Teachers feel undervalued by administrators and districts when professional development sessions are consistently conducted by external consultants. Backyard experts are your district's hidden influencers. Tap teachers and staff to share their knowledge and expertise for their *own* school district, and you may find increased engagement and enthusiasm—and less frustration.

Set High Expectations

All the time. For everyone—students, teachers, parents, decision makers. Even teachers you think aren't willing or students you think aren't capable. Set and communicate high *and* reasonable expectations, provide support and structure to achieve these expectations, and work to create an atmosphere in which everyone can hold one another mutually and transparently accountable. This kind of atmosphere can protect against negativity or distrust. Approaching every day assuming the best in others generates people who achieve their best!

Model Growth Mindset

I highly recommend reading *Mindset: The New Psychology of Success* by Carol Dweck and having all teachers read it too (if they haven't already). Then apply a growth mindset to every student: No matter the subject matter being taught, we can model a belief that everyone has the capacity to stretch their brains. We model this by trying new things ourselves and encouraging appropriate risk in others (for example, making the shift to a leadership culture if it's a completely new way of thinking). We can use language like, "I'm proud of you for trying," and "Even though you get nervous starting new things, I'm here to support you," and "I learned so much from you." A quick internet search will lead you to a variety of great ways leaders and educators have found to structure school and classroom cultures (as well as their personal lives) around a growth mindset.

Be Bold (and Stay Confident)

Growth mindset opens our mind to learning. Effective leaders and educators take it a step further to reward innovation! There's so much pressure for educators to play by rules, but boldness—stepping out of the box, being spontaneous in their classrooms, teaching content using real-life context, avoiding a one-size-fits-all approach—is how educators inspire great leaps in learning. Teachers thrive when their building and district leadership supports this. Preach boldness and *practice it* by stepping out of your comfort zone with colleagues (for example, volunteer to lead a professional development session on something everyone is asking for but hasn't been done) and push students out of their comfort zones (for example, serving as a catalyst or advisor for students who propose new clubs or projects). Future employers and communities will thank you.

Embrace Workplace 2020 Competencies

Today's students will be taking on tomorrow's jobs—jobs that are likely to demand different, higher-order thinking skills than the jobs we know today. Technology will streamline certain tasks, yet many of the industries expected to expand between now and 2026 will depend on human interaction, relationships, and leadership skills.[6] Look again at the list of 2020 workplace skills (page 15) sought by employers and do two things: (1) honestly assess *your own* skills in these areas, and (2) honestly assess how well your school or district cultivates these skills in students (with and without the changes you're implementing to achieve a leadership culture).

---

6. "Occupational Outlook Handbook," Bureau of Labor Statistics (January 30, 2018), www.bls.gov/ooh/most-new-jobs.htm.

When we, as educators, embrace the rapidly changing jobs landscape, we better understand the importance of teaching leadership skills in conjunction with academic content. Personal introspection—asking ourselves if we're leading our schools or teaching content in outdated ways—is one way to assess our own 2020 workplace readiness. Continue to engage a growth mindset by seeking out information you might not associate with K–12 education, like following future workplace trends online by searching terms like "Workplace 2020," "talent economy," and "future workforce." You'll find articles like these:

- "K12, College, and the Workforce: Collaborating to Prepare for Jobs of the Future," National Conference of State Legislators, January 22, 2014 (bit.ly/2IqhEIT)

- "How K–12 Teachers Prepare Students for Skills of the Future," Lauren Dixon, *Talent Economy,* December 1, 2017 (bit.ly/2FVqEqU)

Also look for articles on how to prepare people of all ages, including educators who may want to enter a different industry, such as "5 Big Ways Education Will Change by 2020," by Samantha Cole at the website *Fast Company* (bit.ly/2ur4h6q). And of course, implementing what you've read throughout this book is a great way to address and prevent gaps or deficiencies.

Be Wine, Not the Cork

Wine and people both need breathing room to be their best. Good wine benefits from generous sharing; corks prevent spillage. In people-terms, wine brings forth congeniality, encouraging moving forward freely over roadblocks and hindrances. Corks block good ideas through behaviors like micromanaging or poor communication. Don't like the wine analogy? Then be a river, not a dam.

Speak Last

Listen to what your team has to say. Listen to what students have to say. Listen to where people fall on issues. Synthesize what you hear. And then speak—not with authority but with empathy to find the best solution and the best path to empower classroom and culture change-makers.

Accept Fuzziness

Human behavior is complex; it drives many to seek clean, clear lines wherever possible. Right and wrong, good and bad, winners and losers. The starting line and the finish line. Metrics and data that purport to prove student growth or improvement (even if interpretable from various perspectives). Grades that supposedly show knowledge mastery (or show a student's ability to follow a teacher's or professor's rubric!).

That's why it can be difficult for decision makers to endorse spending school time cultivating leadership and soft skills—those skills are hard to measure or put our finger on. It's obvious when people have them, but data to support their value is hard to come by. Even long-term benefits like better relationships, better public leadership, and better communication skills take many years to play out. Investing in K–12 leadership cultures knowing the positive outcomes are sometimes intangible manifests in a society filled with measurable leadership behaviors in the long run.

Change Lives

In my career, I've been lucky to interact with a diverse range of students and adults of all ages and in many settings. One thing I've learned over and over is that engaging in relationship-driven leadership development inspires people to work well with others *and* to do good work.

With social media making it easy to find and contact people, you may already have former students reaching out to you through Facebook and LinkedIn. For me, it's rewarding to receive messages and read posts that tell of former students' highlights and challenges, to hear their post-graduation stories, and to observe their leadership journeys and career highlights. Students introduce me to their families and sometimes to the recruiter or manager who hired them. Even more, I love reading messages from employers who hired the students—they're usually generous with praise about how the young adult's sense of self, skilled relationship-building, respectful confidence, and coachability (code for leadership skills) made them stand out. When you teach or lead in a school with a leadership culture, you'll recognize that the success of students like these stems from learning to lead while they were in school. Knowing we had a hand in that reminds us of the long-term impact we make.

Imagine how contemporary company executives and politicians might behave differently if their K–12 educational experience had included intentional leadership development with attention to nurturing social intelligence. Imagine how discussions about public policy, social issues, and social-cultural differences might sound if everyone in the conversation had a similar understanding of how each of us has a role and responsibility as a leadership influencer.

If we want a world where our leaders lead deliberately and inclusively, we must *prepare* them to lead deliberately and inclusively, starting in kindergarten. Creating cultures where all students—compliant, rebellious, outlier, or mainstream—learn to recognize their roles as everyday leaders changes lives. And changes life.

PART 3

ADDITIONAL RESOURCES

Creating a Leadership Sticker Chart
(For Classroom Management)

A leadership sticker chart is a method to naturally integrate leadership behaviors and expectations in classrooms with younger students. Students collect stickers on a chart that they can redeem for tokens or tickets, which they can redeem for prizes or other rewards you establish. I've done it where five stickers equal a token, and five tokens can be redeemed for a larger-value ticket to use for the class treasure box or at the end-of-year "store."

Early in the school year, facilitate a discussion with students about how they want others to behave in class. Focus on how everyone can be successful if they agree to shared norms and behave consistently with these. Phrase expectations positively rather than negatively (for example, "Take turns when talking" instead of "No interrupting"). List the expectations on the board, then transfer the list to a large poster board or other durable material (it needs to last all year) to hang prominently in the classroom. On another board, list each child's name with an open row of space following. This is where you'll put the stickers they earn. You might consider doing it in a digital format (something as easy as an Excel spreadsheet does the trick) so you don't have to make new boards once the first one is full.

When I used this format, the kids selected stickers that looked like doggie paw prints. As a result, we referred to the chart as our "Leadership Paw Chart." To earn a paw print, kids need to complete the leadership actions of the various categories the class determined together. The list can change as the year goes on or if certain patterns arise that the class agrees are creating bad vibes (for example, being argumentative or dawdling when cleaning up). Examples of paw-print-worthy leadership actions might include:

- listening the first time
- arriving to school prepared
- having a "can-do" attitude even when things are challenging
- being respectful to one another
- random acts of kindness (self-identified)

- random acts of kindness (recognized by others—earn two paw prints!)
- getting ready for activity transitions, lunch, end of day routines, and so on, without reminders
- cleaning up the classroom without being asked
- cooperating and not being argumentative or talking back to prove a point
- staying calm and resolving differences together (without an adult)
- walking away instead of arguing or trying to be right
- saying yes and being positive
- cooperating with one another—no questions asked and no "buts"
- showing initiative in the classroom and around school
- "Wild Card" (paw print given freely to someone else because of something special they did without being asked or asking to be noticed)
- volunteering to help classmates or teachers

Like certain aspects of leading well, earning paw prints in some categories may be easier than others, but earning five paw prints in the same category won't earn a token or ticket (whatever you use in your classroom). Instead, earning one paw print in five different categories earns a token or ticket. Allow students to collect their tokens every week, or if it works better for you and your group, allow students to wait a few weeks, combine for a maximum number (whatever you determine), and then collect.

Sample School-Based Leadership Day

An efficient and highly impactful way to infuse leadership is to conduct a Leadership Day, a student-driven mini-conference. The sample included here is for an elementary school, with student mentors from a high school. Depending on how you design such an experience, once everyone has been trained, the actual day is conducted primarily by the high school students.

Choosing the Date and Personnel

To begin, identify the date on which to conduct the Leadership Day. You might do it early in the school year as a kickoff to your leadership theme for the year. If conducted later in the year, around or after spring break, it can be used as inspiration to finish the year strong or to launch goals for the following year. A date later in the school year lends itself to leading discussions with the students moving up to another school like middle or high school.

Divide younger students into groups of ten to twelve and assign two teen mentors to each group. It's helpful to partner with a vice principal at the high school from where mentors are being selected. This person will have firsthand knowledge of and relationships with his or her students to make good selections. Ask the high school point person to select a diverse group of students that represents the high school—athletes, academics, quiet leaders, resilient students (those who may have overcome obstacles to reach graduation), college-bound students, those on a career/vocational path, and so on.

When determining student mentors for your highest-grade groups (students transitioning to the new school), select students who are comfortable with and appropriate for serving as panel members during the discussion. The panel is most effective when moderated by a school counselor or other individual trusted by your highest-grade audience, with no other teachers or parents in the room. It's also important to establish that what is discussed remains confidential.

In addition to selecting teen mentors, recruit parent volunteers—one per group. The role of parent volunteers is to assist with keeping younger students on task, address any exclusionary or distracting behavior, and help with debriefing the activities with teen mentors if needed. Other than that, they can serve in the shadows with the small groups. This way, the teen mentors are put into true leadership roles and parents help create an inspirational and encouraging atmosphere for their assigned small group. One teacher from the elementary school should be assigned as a partner to the parent for each group as well.

Arrange to meet with the teen mentors at their high school with plenty of lead time at least once to explain the day and their role. Introduce yourself, build rapport, hand out the schedule, discuss goals and objectives, respond to questions, inspire, and get excited. During this meeting, assign the task of determining an age-appropriate icebreaker to the teen mentors. If they need specific props for the icebreaker, determine who is responsible for getting the items (the students, the high school sponsor, the elementary school). The high school point person should be responsible for permission slips and class release at their school.

Preparing for the Day

One to two weeks prior to the Leadership Day, schedule a full training session for the entire group of teen mentors, parent volunteers, and teachers at the elementary school. During this training session, set up and teach all the activities to everyone. Provide handouts with detailed instructions as well as the overall schedule. Allocate time for parents, teachers, and teen mentors to get to know one another. This training session can typically take two hours or more—treat it as an abbreviated "camp counselor boot camp"!

The activities selected in the sample schedule are similar to initiatives teams may complete at a low ropes course (no high wires, posts, or individual challenges). Teen mentors often have a wealth of ideas too and, if time allows, you might add another session with them at the high school to come up with the activities you want to use.

I recommend surprising the teen mentors with a small token of appreciation at the end of the day. Ten-dollar (or less) gift cards to a favorite fast-food or local restaurant go over well.

For safety reasons, identify ahead of time where high school mentors should park at the elementary school, and communicate this to them during one of the trainings. Suggest (or require) that mentors wear spirit gear from the high school and communicate to them any dress codes (for example, no hats or caps) or behavioral expectations (no gum chewing, no swearing), since the younger kids will notice *everything* they say, do, and wear! Also, require high school mentors to sign in at the elementary school and wear visitor badges to make them easily identifiable. For the sample schedule provided, high school students are asked to eat prior to arriving so they can set up, ask last-minute questions, meet with parent volunteers assigned to their groups, and be ready for the kickoff.

Sample Leadership Day Schedule

12:00–1:00
- High school mentors arrive and set up rooms.
- Parent volunteers arrive and reconnect with mentors assigned to their groups.

1:00–1:15
- All students gather in the gym for kickoff (the principal sets the tone by welcoming the group and previewing the schedule).
- Divide the student body by having previously assigned small groups join their high school mentors at the front. Each group leaves the gym once it has formed, and mentors lead their groups to their first activity room.

For Students in Grades 3–5

1:15–1:30
Create connections in small groups through the name game and an icebreaker; please use the entire 15 minutes.

1:30–2:15
Conduct the first small-group leadership activity and discussion; see specific activity descriptions and discussion questions.

2:15–3:00
Conduct a leadership discussion; two sample theme topics can be found on pages 140–141.

Middle School Transition Activities for Students in Grades 5 or 6

While younger grades are participating in their small-group activities, students in your school's highest grade participate in activities in small groups comprised only of students in their grade.

1:15–2:00

- Conduct the Zapping Maze activity (in the digital content for this book—see page 157 for instructions on how to download; use the version that works best for the age group).

- Emphasize problem-solving, helping friends in sticky situations, appropriate risk-taking, seeing things from different points of view, dealing with peer pressure, teamwork, and communication, all in the context of middle school.

2:00–3:00

Student Mentors Panel Discussion: Everything you want to know about middle school but are afraid to ask

Conduct discussion in a separate, open room without desks, with space that lends itself to casual conversation, such as a school library; start with brief discussion around the leadership day theme and relate it to the transition to middle school.

All Groups, All Grades

3:00–3:15

Return to the gym. Two high school mentors share their leadership insights (what it means to be a leader; examples of how they fill buckets or confront bucket dippers). High school mentors lead a community popular cheer, inserting name of elementary or middle school instead of high school, changing words to include "leaders" if possible; or other energetic closing.

3:15

High school mentors line up in front of room so elementary students can walk past, exchange high fives, and "network" as they leave the room.

3:20

Return to home classrooms

Sample Discussion Theme 1

Discussion Theme: Leaders Who Fill Buckets (Positive Cultures of Leadership)

Mentor Text: *Have You Filled a Bucket Today? A Guide to Daily Happiness* by Carol McCloud

Read the book aloud to the group. Guide the discussion using prompts like these:

- What connections can you make between the story and your life?

- What connections can you make between the story and what happens at your school?

- What are some examples about what can fill people's buckets? (Examples include: positive compliments, heartfelt attention, being authentic and specific about what you say and do with someone, positive self-talk, noticing others, standing up for others.) Emphasize that *authentic* compliments (bucket fillers) don't focus on someone's looks or other physical traits but rather on someone's spirit, attitude, or contribution.

- What do *you* need to fill your bucket?

- How do you fill your *own* bucket? (Talk about the idea of not waiting for or counting on others to fill your bucket and the importance of making your own happiness.)

- What do you do when your bucket feels empty?

- How can you tell if someone else feels like their bucket is empty?

- How do you stop yourself from being a "bucket dipper"?

- What can you do when you see or hear a bucket dipping?

After the discussion, pass out two sheets of paper cut into the shape of buckets (or two copies of a page with the shape of a bucket drawn on it) to each student, asking everyone to write down examples of bucket fillers on one, such as "Invite someone new to play with you on the playground" or "Tell someone they had a great answer in class." Have them write a specific example of positive self-talk on the other bucket, such as "You can ACE this test!" Collect the sheets of paper in 5-gallon buckets. Hang the paper buckets around school after Leadership Day.

Sample Discussion Theme 2

Discussion Theme: Empathetic Leadership (treating others with care)

Mentor Text: *Do Unto Otters: A Book About Manners* by Laurie Keller

Read the book aloud to the group, then guide the discussion using prompts like these:

- What connections can you make between the story and your life?
- What examples can you think of where you did "acts of service" for others?
- How might you want others to do acts of service for you?
- What connections can you make between the story and what happens at our school?
- What are some examples of ways you "do unto otters"? (Examples include: positive compliments, heartfelt attention to others, being authentic and specific about what you say and do with someone, positive self-talk, noticing others, standing up for others, following through on group projects, and so forth.)
- In what ways can people be more thoughtful and intentional with how they treat others?
- The book brings up apologizing and forgiving when rabbit calls the otter "snotter" and apologizes. What's the difference between saying something that's truly funny to others and saying something that's sarcastic followed by "I'm just kidding"? How can humor be used in positive ways with one another?
- How can you demonstrate friendliness with others, even if you may not consider someone a friend (or you don't care for them)?
- Which is harder to do—be kind or be mean? What steps can everyone at our school take to elevate kindness above meanness?

After the discussion, pass out a sheet of construction paper to each student, asking everyone to write down examples of ways they can "do unto otters" or ways others can "do unto them," such as "Invite someone new to play with me on the playground," "Tell someone they had a great answer in class," and "Be true to your word." (Leave completed pages in the room; these will be picked up.)

Master Schedule

After establishing groups—including the activities, student leaders, and adult chaperones for each—as well as the rooms and times for each group's activities, your schedule will look something like the following examples. Depending on the number of groups and the amount of space you have, choose several activities and set up the activities in multiple rooms. Schedule groups in rotations as illustrated in the following table. Consider making tables like these to keep everyone organized. All activities (in italics) can be found in the digital content for this book. See page 157 for instructions on how to download.

Grades 3–5				
Group	**First Activity and Leadership Discussion** 1:15–2:30	**Second Activity** 2:30–3:00	**Student Leaders**	**Adults**
1	Name game of your choosing Icebreaker of your choosing *Candlestick Relay* Leadership discussion [Room #]	*House of Cards* [Room #]	[name 1] [name 2]	[teacher name] [parent name]
2	Name game Icebreaker *House of Cards* Leadership discussion [Room #]	*Olympic Rings* [Room #]	[name 1] [name 2]	[teacher name] [parent name]
3	Name game Icebreaker *Olympic Rings* Leadership discussion [Room #]	*Candlestick Relay* [Room #]	[name 1] [name 2]	[teacher name] [parent name]

Middle School Transition (Grades 5 or 6)				
Group	First Activity 1:15–2:00	Second Activity All Groups Together 2:00–3:00	Student Leaders	Adults
1	*Zapping Maze* [Room #]	Student Mentors Panel Discussion [Room #]	[name 1] [name 2]	[teacher name] [parent name]
2	*Zapping Maze* [Room #]	Student Mentors Panel Discussion [Room #]	[name 1] [name 2]	[teacher name] [parent name]
3	*Zapping Maze* [Room #]	Student Mentors Panel Discussion [Room #]	[name 1] [name 2]	[teacher name] [parent name]

Leadership Lesson Plans Aligned to Academic Subjects

Each lesson in this section is structured around the interactive leadership activity identified in the lesson title and expanded with mentor texts and additional instructions to ground it more firmly in the academic area (noted by "Standards Alignment"). All leadership activities are available in the digital content for this book. See page 157 for instructions on how to download.

Most of these lessons can be completed in a typical class period (45–50 minutes). You may decide to give certain content or discussion more time, depending on the age of students, subject area, how the lesson is embedded in the curriculum sequence, and other factors. As presented, most of the lessons are geared toward elementary-age children, but they're easily modified, extended, and enriched for older audiences.

LESSON 1: SQUEEZE

Standards Alignment: ELA–Speaking & Listening/Writing, Math, Science, Physical Education

Mentor Text: "Submission Guidelines," *The First Line* (bit.ly/2omWf9K) and "First Lines," Short Story Ideas (bit.ly/2pfpbRL)

Learning Objectives: Probability (if used for Math/Science), First Line Stories (if used for ELA)

Leadership Lessons: Teamwork, Verbal and Nonverbal Communication, Problem-Solving

Audience: Grades 4 and up

Steps

1. Facilitate the "Squeeze" activity as directed. To debrief for probability, discuss principles of probability related to flipping a coin. To debrief for ELA, discuss the impact of one person knowing what's happening and then having to pass along that message to others.

2. *If teaching as a probability lesson:* Introduce probability, fractions, or related concepts relevant to the age group with which you're working. Math Goodies has a variety of methods (bit.ly/2tMclAb). After you've introduced the topic, divide students into groups of three. Pass out nontransparent paper lunch bags filled with 3 red poker chips (or similar plastic item), 3 blue chips, and 3 white chips. Ask each group to create a simple table with three columns: Column 1 will show which draw they're on; Column 2 will show what color was drawn from the bag; Column 3 will show the probability of each color being drawn next (for example, red=30% blue=25% white=60%). Without looking in the bag, have the first student choose a chip from the bag and have the group calculate the probability of picking a red, blue, or white chip next. Have a second student remove a plastic chip from the bag; again, have the group calculate the probability of choosing each color. Continue until the bag is empty.

3. *If teaching as an ELA lesson:* Assign individually or to students in small groups. Give the same first line of a story to the entire class. Have one student from each group write the first line on a sheet of paper or in a word processing document. Have the individual or group craft the rest of the story. This can be given as an in-class exercise or as homework. If you want, extend the lesson with older students by having individuals or teams submit to *The First Line* literary journal.

LESSON 2: PUZZLE

Standards Alignment: Math, ELA–Speaking & Listening

Learning Objectives: Geometric 2-D Shapes

Leadership Lessons: Working with Others, Communication, Problem-Solving

Audience: Grades 3 and up

Steps

1. Facilitate the "Puzzle" activity as instructed.

2. Lead a related lesson of your choice on geometry, specifically 2-D designs.

LESSON 3: CAMPAIGN TEAMS

This lesson is best conducted over two to three class sessions.

Standards Alignment: Social Studies, ELA–Speaking & Listening/Writing

Mentor Text: "Tips from the Insiders: How to Write a Political Speech" (adapted from Scholastic's *Voice*, bit.ly/2yia4gp)

Learning Objectives: Current Events, Civics, Contextual Writing, Public Speaking

Leadership Lessons: Working with Others, Setting and Achieving Goals, Public Speaking, First Impressions, and Personal Polish

Audience: Grades 6 and up

Steps

1. Facilitate the "Campaign Teams" activity as instructed. Hand out or have students digitally access the tips on writing a political speech. As a group project during or after class time, assign each team to write a speech and to select an individual to present it.

2. As an extension or homework assignment following the campaigning, ask each student to write a winning or concession speech (randomly assign which speech each student is to do).

LESSON 4: WHAT'S IN A NAME?

Standards Alignment: ELA–Writing and Language, Social Studies, National Service Learning Standards

Mentor Text: Excerpt from *Romeo and Juliet*: Act II, Scene II

Learning Objectives: Literature Interpretation, Understanding Stereotypes and Prejudice, Setting Tone for Service Projects

Leadership Lessons: First Impressions, Qualities of Leadership, Building Inclusion, Empathy, and Understanding

Audience: Grades 7 and up

Steps

1. Ask students to read the *Romeo and Juliet* excerpt independently. Briefly discuss before facilitating the "What's in a Name?" activity as directed.

2. If possible, connect this lesson to an SEL lesson or a discussion on empathy and inclusion. This is also a good lesson for training student mentors.

LESSON 5: HOUSE OF CARDS

Standards Alignment: Math, Science (your state standards)

Mentor Text: the game Tetris (Electronic Arts) or Minecraft (Mojang) (online or app)

Learning Objectives: Physics, Estimating

Leadership Lessons: Working with Others, Nonverbal Communication, Problem-Solving, Creative Thinking

Audience: Grades 4 and up

Steps

1. Facilitate the "House of Cards" activity as directed.

2. Lead an age-appropriate lesson of your choice in one of the following areas: physics (related to structure, weight, shape, and balance); introduction to building engineering; calculating area of irregular shapes; or visual spatial (estimating space and positions).

3. Extend the lesson using Tetris or Minecraft, both of which reinforce patterns, visual-spatial recognition, and geometric concepts (translation, reflection, and rotation).

LESSON 6: OLYMPIC RINGS

Standards Alignment: Science

Learning Objectives: Motion, Force, and Trajectory (Physics)

Leadership Lessons: Communication, Teamwork, Trust, Problem-Solving, Qualities of Leaders

Audience: Grades 4 and up

Steps

1. Facilitate the "Olympic Rings" activity as directed.

2. Debrief for physics by discussing principles of trajectory and motion related to swinging the rings (or if using the floor alternative, tossing bean bags). If you prefer, teach the academic lesson first as a prelude to using the physics concepts.

3. Introduce motion, force, and trajectory concepts relevant to the age group with which you're working. EdGalaxy has a variety of creative lessons for elementary and middle school students (www.edgalaxy.com/search?q =physics). LearningScience.org also has a rich collection of interactive lessons specific to force and motion (www.learningscience.org/psc2bmo tionforces.htm). For older students, consider a direct correlation to the Winter Olympics (nyti.ms/2vv7KDp).

LESSON 7: FLOATING PIPELINE

Standards Alignment: Science

Learning Objectives: Rolling Motion, Torque, and Angular Momentum (Physics)

Leadership Lessons: Communication, Creative Thinking, Teamwork

Audience: Grades 4 and up

Steps

1. Facilitate the "Floating Pipeline" activity as directed.

2. Debrief for physics by discussing principles of rolling motion, torque, or angular momentum related to tipping the pipes and movement of students to keep the path going. If you prefer, teach the academic lesson first as a prelude to using the physics concepts.

3. Introduce rolling motion, torque, or angular momentum concepts relevant to the age group with which you're working. TeachEngineering.org has a diverse collection of lessons for all grades. Under the "Show Curriculum" tab, click on "Subject Areas," then click on "Physics," and then search for "Rolling Motion," "Torque," or "Angular Momentum" in the "narrow results" search window.

Sample Parent/Community Member Handout

Building a Leadership Culture at [Name of school/district]

Leadership is something at which everyone can succeed. Being a leader and acting with leadership intentions doesn't require holding certain positions or needing to be showy; being a leader can be demonstrated in little things people do every day:

- speaking up in class with a unique perspective
- picking up the piece of trash that everyone else walks by
- standing up for a friend who's being bullied
- doing the right thing, even when others push you to do something else
- getting good grades
- inspiring friends in positive ways
- making good decisions
- resolving conflicts in positive ways and seeking help when it's needed
- volunteering (in the community, in a place of worship, in a club, on a sports team, and so on)

According to the W.K. Kellogg Foundation, an important contributor to research on leadership climate and environment at schools (and in communities), students attending schools where the climate emphasizes leadership experience the following benefits:

- increased commitment to service and volunteerism
- improved communication skills
- higher sense of personal and social responsibility
- increased sense of civic/social/political efficacy
- improved self-esteem
- improved problem-solving ability

- increased civic/social/political activity
- increased sense of being galvanized for action
- increased desire for change
- improved ability to vision
- improved ability to be issue-focused
- improved conflict resolution skills
- improved likelihood of sharing power

Independent of the Kellogg research, information collected from various middle and high school youth leadership programs and classes show that students who participate in leadership activities at school or in their communities have:

- better attendance rates
- higher achievement and graduation rates
- greater confidence in resolving conflicts
- increased involvement in decision-making processes
- increased interest in community service and "giving back" to others
- stronger ownership for school-related projects, programs, and efforts

Based on this information, we can deduce that leadership education starting in elementary grades will strengthen and sustain the outcomes identified in older students.

Leadership education goes beyond "character education" by promoting the ability to make a difference through taking individual and group action. Leadership education develops measurable skills and attitudes such as decision-making, acting ethically, communication, teamwork, critical thinking, and empathy and builds character-based behaviors such as responsibility, dependability, courtesy, and respect.

Our school has thoughtfully made the decision to make leadership development a priority. Building lifelong leaders demands consistent role modeling, leadership-focused discussions, and commitment from all adults. We'll provide you with resources along the way because we believe leadership can't be achieved without having parents, caretakers, and other significant adults in our students' lives as partners.

Suggested Further Reading

"Blended Learning for Leadership: The CCL Approach" by Ron Rabin (Center for Creative Leadership, 2014)

"Global Human Capital Trends 2015: Leading in the New World of Work" edited by Josh Bersin, Dimple Agarwal, Bill Pelster, and Jeff Schwartz (Deloitte University Press, 2015)

Learning Leadership: The Five Fundamentals of Becoming an Exemplary Leader by James. M. Kouzes and Barry Z. Posner (Wiley, 2016)

Mindset: The New Psychology of Success by Carol S. Dweck (Random House, 2016)

Social Intelligence: The New Science of Success by Karl Albrecht (Wiley, 2009)

"How to Give a Killer Presentation" by Chris Anderson, *Harvard Business Review* (June 2013), hbr.org/2013/06/how-to-give-a-killer-presentation

Collaborative for Academic and Social Emotional Learning (CASEL), casel.org

"What 'Transforming the Workforce' Says About Developing Children's Social-Emotional Skills" by Aaron Loewenberg, *New America Weekly* (Dec. 12, 2016), www.newamerica.org/education-policy/edcentral/what-transforming-work -force-says-about-developing-childrens-social-emotional-skills

Index

To download the reproducible forms and other digital content for this book,
visit **freespirit.com/leadership-forms**. Use the password **2succeed**.

About the Author

Mariam G. MacGregor, M.S., is director of Employee Engagement and Organizational Strategy at Texas Christian University (TCU) and a nationally recognized leadership consultant who works with schools (K–12 and higher education), nonprofit agencies, faith groups, and communities interested in developing meaningful, sustainable leadership efforts for kids, teens, and young adults. Mariam lived in Colorado for many years, where she served as the school counselor and coordinator of leadership programs at an alternative high school and received  honorable mention for Counselor of the Year. She also worked with college student leaders at Syracuse University, Santa Clara University, Metropolitan State College of Denver, and TCU, and was the youth volunteer trainer for Night Lights (a respite care program that serves families of kids with special needs) and EPIC Mentors (a program started by one of her sons at his elementary school that pairs peer mentors with kids with learning challenges). She lives in Texas with her husband and three kind kids. Learn more about Mariam at mariammacgregor.com.

Other Everyday Leadership Resources

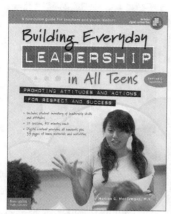

Building Everyday Leadership in All Teens
Promoting Attitudes and Actions for Respect and Success
(Revised & Updated Edition)

by Mariam G. MacGregor, M.S.

For teachers and youth workers, grades 6–12.

*240 pp.; paperback; 8½" x 11"
Digital content includes reproducible handouts and lots of bonus materials.*

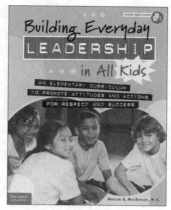

Building Everyday Leadership in All Kids
An Elementary Curriculum to Promote Attitudes and Actions for Respect and Success

by Mariam G. MacGregor, M.S.

For teachers, grades K–6.

*176 pp.; paperback; 8½" x 11"
Digital content includes customizable reproducible forms.*

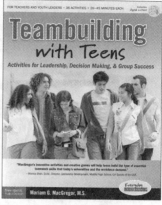

Teambuilding with Teens
Activities for Leadership, Decision Making, & Group Success

by Mariam G. MacGregor, M.S.

For teachers and youth workers, grades 6–12.

*192 pp.; paperback; 8½" x 11"
Digital content includes all of the reproducible forms from the book.*

Everyday Leadership
Attitudes and Actions for Respect and Success
(A Guidebook for Teens)

by Mariam G. MacGregor, M.S.

For ages 11 & up.

144 pp.; paperback; 7" x 9"

Everyday Leadership Cards
Writing and Discussion Prompts

by Mariam G. MacGregor, M.S.

For grades 6–12.

60 cards; two-color; 3" x 4½"

Leadership Lessons In a Jar®
Daily Wisdom for Personal and Professional Success

For ages 16 & up.

101 cards.

Other Great Resources from Free Spirit

by Jonathan C. Erwin

For administrators, teachers, and counselors, grades K–12.

200 pp.; paperback; 8½" x 11" Digital content includes customizable forms from the book.

by Maurice J. Elias, Ph.D., and Steven E. Tobias, Psy.D.

For teachers and counselors of grades 5–9.

192 pp.; paperback; 8½" x 11" Digital content includes reproducible forms from the book.

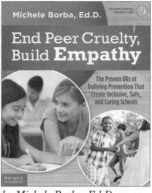

by Michele Borba, Ed.D.

For administrators, teachers, counselors, youth leaders, bullying prevention teams, parents of children in grades K–8.

288 pp.; paperback; 7¼" x 9¼" Digital content includes customizable forms from the book and a PDF presentation for use in professional development. Free PLC / Book Study Guide available at freespirit.com / PLC.

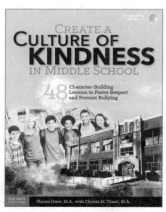

by Naomi Drew, M.A., with Christa M. Tinari, M.A.

For middle school educators.

272 pp.; paperback; 8½" x 11" Digital content includes customizable student handouts from the book.

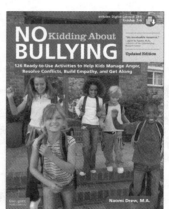

by Naomi Drew, M.A.

For teachers and counselors of grades 3–6.

304 pp.; paperback; 8½" x 11" Digital content includes reproducible forms and bonus material.

Interested in purchasing multiple quantities and receiving volume discounts?
Contact edsales@freespirit.com or call 1.800.735.7323 and ask for Education Sales.

Many Free Spirit authors are available for speaking engagements, workshops, and keynotes. Contact speakers@freespirit.com or call 1.800.735.7323.

For pricing information, to place an order, or to request a free catalog, contact:

Free Spirit Publishing Inc. • 6325 Sandburg Road, Suite 100 • Minneapolis, MN 55427-3674
toll-free 800.735.7323 • local 612.338.2068 • fax 612.337.5050
help4kids@freespirit.com • www.freespirit.com